finding shelter

PORTRAITS OF LOVE, HEALING, AND SURVIVAL

JESSE FREIDIN

GUILFORD, CONNECTICUT

An imprint of Globe Pequot

Distributed by NATIONAL BOOK NETWORK

British Library Cataloguing in Publication Information Available

Library of Congress Cataloging-in-Publication Data

ISBN 978-1-4930-2509-1 (hardcover)
ISBN 978-1-4930-2510-7 (e-book)

∞™ The paper used in this publication meets the minimum requirements of American National
Standard for Information Sciences—Permanence of Paper for Printed Library Materials,
ANSI/NISO Z39.48-1992.

This book is dedicated to Madalin Bernard, the late director of Used Dogs Rescue, and every other animal shelter and rescue volunteer that we've lost over the years. May their beautiful spirits and unending dedication continue to give a voice to the voiceless, inspire us to work as one, fill us with enormous hope, and remind us to always balance the dark with the light.

contents

acknowledgments

This book would not have been possible had it not been for the thousands of people who supported my Kickstarter campaign. The list is too long to name you all, but I deeply appreciate every single dollar that every one of you gave. You made this book a reality.

Tamara Silva helped me coordinate the very first *Finding Shelter* test shoot at NKLA's (No Kill Los Angeles) beautiful shelter in Los Angeles. Those portraits—all done with a large-format 4·5 view camera and black-and-white instant film—were instrumental in helping me fine-tune my creative process. Clearly, the 4·5 was not the right camera for the job, but those were some great test shots.

Jill Meredith graciously curated all the portraits in this book with her museum-trained eye.

Thanks to Siobhan O'Brien for perfectly naming all my creative projects, and Jenni Heller for transcribing nearly one hundred interviews. Thanks to Daphne Gottlieb and Rachel Welles for your editing expertise.

I'm lucky to have the two best assistants in the world: Amanda Brauning and Connor Cook. Thank you for going on this epic road trip with me, for your consistent hard work and inhumanely long hours, and for your unending friendship. And thanks for making sure none of us took home any dogs.

Sara Engel, your help got me off on the right foot, and I truly appreciate it.

My good friend Sarah Deragon coached me through preparing and executing a successful crowdfunding campaign.

Ana Bustilloz at the spcaLA was gracious enough to let me photograph her volunteers *and* make my Kickstarter video at her shelter.

I truly appreciate the time and attention of the following volunteer coordinator and shelter managers: Sarah Luce, Kasey Spain, Amanda Wood, Rose Janice, Ramon Herrera, Heather Dinneen, Sena Fitzpatrick, Deborah Tittle and Linda Chute, Elodie Lorenz, Terry Bissaillon, Cindy Chapman, Lauraine Merlini, Jan Dukes, Debbie Vogel, Allegra Haldeman, Madalin Bernard, Richard Knighton, Lesley Brog, Donna Reynolds, Bunny Rosenberg, Mia Gyzander, Hilary Gillespie, Ande Cira, Alex Caswell, and Larkin O'Toole.

And lastly, thank you to my agent Anna Olswanger, my editor Holly Rubino, and everyone at Lyons Press for having such faith in this project.

introduction

For the past few years, I have watched my colleagues in the dog photography world get caught up in photographing adoptable shelter animals—and what a great trend to be caught up in! It is incredibly generous and hugely important work. It also tips the balance to survival for so many animals. But what I feel is missing from that trend is a wider view of the shelter system—one that incorporates the human aspect of shelter work. Without the volunteers, our nation's animal shelters simply would not function.

Shelter volunteers are amazing people. They are selfless, dedicated, and deeply attached to their cause. They are looking to give their love to something outside of themselves and in return receive the powerful, unspoken love of a shelter dog. Though rarely discussed within the animal welfare system, volunteers find an environment of support and friendship in their relationships with these animals, making the shelter a place for humans and animals to heal together. *Finding Shelter* gives volunteers an opportunity to tell their own stories, in their own words—all of which focus on how healing and joyful this work truly is.

I started this project in the beginning of 2014 and spent a year driving up and down the California coast on my own dime, convincing shelters and rescue groups that I had a story to tell and that they could trust me. As an artist and storyteller, my first concern is always that the community I am immersing myself in believes I will advocate for it and portray the experiences of its members honestly. Even though I'd been working in the dog world as a photographer for nearly ten years, I wasn't a volunteer. I was an outsider, and some people were understandably a little wary. Although I was originally told that shelter volunteers would be too shy to face my camera, that is certainly not what I found. It was clear that the animal shelter world was ready for someone to reinterpret what their work was actually about and to help show a kinder, softer side of it and someone to finally talk about how volunteer work was a two-way street—that the animals were having an equally positive impact on the people who worked to save them. The old image of the downtrodden animal shelter as dirty, sad, and full of "bad" dogs was not serving anyone anymore, and I was determined to change that.

This inspired me to drive across the country in the summer of 2015 so that I could tell a much broader story. I turned to crowdfunding and within a matter of days raised enough money to cover my expenses, as well as afford three amazing assistants. The project went viral and was picked up by media sources all over the world. To me, this was a sign that this story needed to be told. And, of course, I was immensely grateful.

My intention when driving across the country was to work with a very eclectic group of shelters and rescue organizations. So I reached out to some that had an incredible amount of financial support with state-of-the-art facilities and a no-kill policy. I also reached out to those that had such little funding that their buildings were crumbling, but that still managed to save the lives of hundreds of dogs each year.

To keep the portraits realistic, I relied on natural light. I let dogs wear leashes and volunteers wear dog hair because these portraits are not glamour shots—they are honest representations of the animal welfare world. Every shelter presented new challenges. Was there an open room we could work in? Was there enough light for my camera? Would we be in the way? The circus act of creating a clean photo studio within a busy animal shelter was one of the most challenging and exciting parts of this project. This energy fueled me and my assistants to get it right on the first try at each new location.

While I was on the road, the politics of the animal rescue world did not matter to me. Though so many people today are outraged at the reality of euthanasia, the fact is that it is impossible to save every animal that comes through the shelter system. It's a numbers game, and the numbers are stacked against us. The pressure to save every single homeless animal in the world is a heavy burden to bear, and one that has caused us to lose too many volunteers and advocates. Though millions are euthanized every year, however, that number is slowly decreasing and will continue to do so as long as we dedicate ourselves to rehabilitating shelter animals so that they can more easily find their forever families. We can solve this epidemic of pet overpopulation by not giving up on shelter animals and by doing all that we can to erase the negative connotations associated with a shelter pet, as well as educating the public about responsible pet ownership and supporting responsible owners who need assistance keeping their animals out of the shelter system. This means providing free or low-cost vaccines and spay/neuter options, basic training, and quality food assistance programs in every city. I truly believe that there are solutions, and volunteers are our first line of defense. I believe we can *change* every shelter animal, if not *save* every shelter animal.

What I found out on my journey was that animals need us. We humans have overbred our pets, to their own detriment, and now we have an overpopulation crisis on our hands. It is our responsibility to fix this. Most people are unable to step back and truly see this epidemic as something that affects every corner of our country and every community. By viewing the problem from coast to coast,

I was able to get a deeper understanding of how our nation's volunteers are handling this issue.

My hope is that within the pages of this book you'll see the true humanity and ethos of the animal welfare system—and the resiliency of its animals. You'll see the endless joy and hope that lies in the faces and souls of our nation's volunteers. Without their incredibly powerful work, we would be living in a country literally overrun by abandoned animals. And that is a reality none of us wants to face.

So, let this work move you. Let it inspire you to go out and adopt your own perfect shelter dog, or even take the first steps toward becoming a volunteer at your local shelter. Every action toward helping a shelter animal has such a deep impact not only on their lives but on ours, as well.

the volunteers

Volunteers spend their lives thinking about how they can keep just one more dog from getting euthanized at the animal shelter. They speak for those who cannot speak, pick up the pieces for abandoned animals who have been let down by previous owners or unfortunate circumstances, and do whatever it takes to heal the deepest of wounds. Without volunteers, our nation's animal shelter system simply would not exist. Their love and beauty are unmatched, and their pride is almost tangible.

When I moved back to Richmond I got my first rescue dog, Maya, a pittie mix. I began volunteering for the rescue that she came from, and that's how I ended up seeing where the shelter animals come from.

When I moved to Philadelphia, Maya got cancer and passed away. I realized that volunteering and getting to spend time with the animals at ACCT was really like free therapy for me. Instead of sitting around and mourning her loss, I decided to do something positive for other shelter animals, and they in turn did something positive for me.

People always ask me how I can volunteer at a kill shelter. I think there's such a need because the animals have to be here anyway. Why do we punish the animals for possibly having to be put down? It's out of their control anyway. Why not come in here and make their days a little better, and work hard to get them out into the community and get them out of here?

Once you volunteer, you quickly become an ambassador for animal rescue when you meet people. Strangers are always proud to talk about their rescue dogs—it's like a club. There's a big misconception among people who get puppies from breeders. They'll say, "We got a puppy from a breeder because we wanted to know what we were getting. We didn't want a dog that had baggage or issues." People ascribe characteristics to animals that aren't necessarily there. It's fear based. Everything is fear based because we're afraid of what we don't know. Maya broke the stereotype of a shelter dog because even though there was a real question mark on her history, she was so amazing. I'm sure other people adopt dogs for the same reason, because they want to prove that stereotype wrong. There's a lot of pride that goes along with that.

VOLUNTEER Linda Morrow

DOG Rocky

RESCUE GROUP Montgomery Humane Society (Montgomery, Alabama)

Back in 1998, when my daughter was a junior in high school and my son was in about seventh grade, we decided that we all needed to do some community service. We came to the shelter because we've always loved animals and we've always had adopted or rescued animals. We came out here and started working where we could. With children, it's a little bit difficult because you can't just walk in and start walking dogs—some of them will run away with you! We started walking the easier dogs and then went into pet therapy. We'd go into the nursing homes and let the patients see the adoptable shelter puppies. Occasionally we would even take kittens.

At first I was too scared to even enter the shelter. I told them, "I can't possibly go in there." The staff understood that and said, "We'll just have them out here by the front door ready for you." It was a slow progression, but once you reach a certain point, you just go all in—either dedicate yourself to the animals, or don't even bother. I started out too scared to even go inside the shelter, and now I'm working in the back!

My kids are grown now, and they have their own dogs that they've adopted from this shelter as adults.

VOLUNTEER Crystal Masingale

DOG Girl

RESCUE GROUP McKinley County Humane Society (Gallup, New Mexico)

I've been fostering animals at McKinley for about a year and a half now. The number of strays around here was what got me started. Just seeing the number of dogs running around on the side of road, starving or dead—it was terrible.

After moving back to Gallup, I saw a dog sitting on the curb with his head down, emaciated, completely defeated, and covered in mange. He was just begging somebody, "Save me, save me." We pulled over, and I sat there for half an hour trying to get him to come to me. That's when I decided I couldn't keep ignoring this any longer. That's when I started fostering dogs.

The work is so exhausting, but you have to do it because without us, they would die. You can't save them all—we know that. You just have to focus on the ones you *did* save, the ones you *did* get out, and all the good that you've done. I think I've had eighty-seven foster dogs come and go through our house this year. When you foster, you really feel like you're doing something, like you're giving back.

Fostering these dogs helps my girls learn how to love. They learn that even if something seems broken, it still deserves a chance. They understand that it's not all about *you*. They learn to be giving people, to not be selfish. I'll tell my daughter, "Well, this dog's leaving on transport in the morning." She'll always give the dogs a goodbye hug and kiss before they go. Then she says, "You go find your forever home. You be good for your new mom and dad." Sometimes people will ask her, "Oh, do you miss so-and-so?" And she'll say, "No, she found a good home now. She has her own family."

VOLUNTEER Richard Loosemore

DOG Dixie

RESCUE GROUP El Paso Animal Services (El Paso, Texas)

I've been volunteering for six months. It was therapy for me at first, because being with dogs has always helped me with my disabilities. But in a sense I'm helping them and they're helping me, so it's really a nice trade-off. I love coming here every day. If I'm in a bad mood, I'll just come to the shelter. I know it's well worth it, because these dogs need homes. I'd take every one of them if I could.

It's a huge sense of pride, a huge sense of accomplishment, to see how many dogs you can actually get out of the shelter and into the community. I always try to match the perfect dog with the perfect family with the perfect home. Seeing them get adopted makes me really happy. Rescue dogs are so appreciative—they can tell that you rescued them, so you already start off on the right foot.

When I came back from my first deployment to Iraq, I got my Saint Bernard. She came down with parvo at ten weeks old. I nursed her all the way back to health, so we've been through a lot together. After that I put her into therapy dog training. She's always had this very special place in my heart. She comes with me to the shelter to help pick out every dog I pull into my Bully Breed rescue, which I've been running here in El Paso for the past few years. She makes sure that we don't just pull the best dogs, but the dogs that need the most help coming out of their shells. Between the time we take them out of the kennel and the time we get them back to the house, their spirits have improved. They're so much better. They're so much happier. They just know they're finally going to be family dogs.

VOLUNTEER Paige MacNeil

DOG Jacks

RESCUE GROUP The Little Guild of Saint Francis
(West Cornwall, Connecticut)

My mom mentioned the Little Guild camp program to me because we adopted our cat from here a few months ago. That's how I got interested in working with the shelter animals. After I went to their spring break camp, the Little Guild asked me to help out at some shelter events.

I like helping the animals—it makes me feel good inside. And I like helping the community, too. It felt good being the only kid from the spring break camp they asked to become a volunteer. It makes me feel special that they chose me to do this.

When I come to the shelter, they don't always have a specific job for me to do, so I usually go care for a cat. I'll pet it and brush it for a while. I still like doing that, because I know I'm helping people, and cats. When we adopted my cat, she was so tiny that I thought I was going to drop her or break her. When we got her home, I put her down, and she hid behind the couch because she was so scared. Then she got used to everything. When I come here, I look at all the kittens and think about how much bigger my cat is now, which means that she's grown since she left the shelter.

I'm learning that different animals need different things. I know that some cats don't like being petted in places like their tail or their head, and some cats do. And some dogs don't like being petted there, either. I'm gonna have a couple dogs when I grow up, and I'm probably gonna volunteer here like I do now.

VOLUNTEER Lesley Brog, director

DOG Kona

RESCUE GROUP Wags and Walks Rescue (Los Angeles, California)

I started Wags and Walks Rescue in 2011 after watching so many friendly, adoptable dogs get euthanized simply because of overcrowding.

I wanted Wags and Walks to feel like a real community. Everybody wants to be part of something really big. Everybody here becomes a family member to us, and we just continue to grow. I don't know if we've lost one single volunteer in all these years. We end up at each other's baby showers and weddings, and the relationships that have come out of this group are something I could have never even dreamed of.

When you're working together for a cause that's important to you, there's a bond that you share. The people who gravitate toward this kind of work have positive outlooks. It's not the "poor me" and "how sad" kind of people. We're driven by inspiration. When it gets hard, we pick each other up. Then we move forward with solutions. That's why we save more dogs than any other group each year. We've got each other's backs, and we've got a support system.

Our new slogan is "Bringing Happiness Home." I really believe it goes both ways. I originally thought that we volunteers bring happiness to the dogs, but then I realized that we actually bring happiness to the adopters' lives, too. When people adopt dogs from us, their relationships get stronger. Single people meet more people. Everyone gets more exercise, and they don't feel lonely anymore. I believe that through rescue and adoption we're changing the world equally for the dog and the person. Wags and Walks is now the fastest-growing rescue in the nation. We've grown from saving 50 dogs in our first year in 2011 to saving more than 800 amazing dogs in 2016.

I plan on being a veterinarian when I graduate high school, but right now I'm the kennel staff—I wash the animals and sometimes I get to help out with the spay and neuter surgeries.

I foster, too. I've fostered probably twenty to thirty animals over the past two years. Sometimes the animals in here carry diseases, and the really young babies can catch the diseases. I don't want to see them get sick and then get put down, so I usually take the young ones home and foster them.

It's important for the animals to feel that there's somebody there. To them you're their forever. What keeps me going is the fact that you see them become healthier and you see them get better homes. I just don't want to see them running around on the streets pregnant with puppies or on the side of the road anymore.

VOLUNTEERS Andretta Sampson and her daughter Shaidae Boyd

DOG Snoopy and Mellow

RESCUE GROUP Animal Care and Control Team Philly
(Philadelphia, Pennsylvania)

Shaidae: I am a senior at the Philadelphia Military Academy. For part of our senior project this year, we had to pick a group to volunteer with. I chose to do my senior research paper on animal cruelty, so I came here to volunteer with the animals.

Andretta: I brought her in for her orientation. I sat through it, and, you know, at first I wasn't going to bother volunteering at all. But after we went through the orientation process, I thought, *I can do this. I can help and contribute because there's so much going on with these animals and people are cruel to them.* Now she's here seven days a week and I'm here six. We come early in the morning, and we stay for a full day. We do the kittens. We do the dogs. We do it all.

Shaidae: I love being around the animals. I like making a difference with them. Not a lot of people get to take them out, and not a lot of people really look into what they go through. I get to learn so much about each animal. I want to be a veterinarian, so I get to learn how to take care of them here, too.

Andretta: Knowing that these pets aren't constantly caged up—that they're taken out and given affection—that makes me so happy. It's an unselfish act that you can do. Your time costs you nothing to give. People think that doing this is so hard, but it's not, and it makes all the difference in the world. I come in here and give the animals time, attention, affection, and that makes me happy. That makes me feel good as a person.

Shaidae: I come here after school. This week I'm off from school, so I'll be here every day.

VOLUNTEER Ginger Phillabaum

DOG Jackson

RESCUE GROUP Montgomery Humane Society (Montgomery, Alabama)

I have been volunteering here for about a year and a half. I love animals. I always thought that if I came to the shelter I'd break down and cry. I was sure I just wouldn't be able to do it. I *did* cry the first time. But I don't live in a situation where I can have a lot of dogs, so this is my way of taking care of them the best I can. I want to give back as much as I can to the community.

It's very satisfying helping somebody or something that cannot help itself. This is where the animals find the love that they deserve and that they need. I'm just thankful to be able do that for them.

VOLUNTEER Kriss Harrigan

DOG Jack

RESCUE GROUP Golden Retriever Club of Greater Los Angeles Rescue
(Los Angeles, California)

I have always had a strong love for animals, but especially dogs and cats. The unconditional love and nourishment that comes from being around dogs really gives me the sense that today matters. Volunteering seems to heighten that sense. We're nurturing another species, and then we can watch these dogs bring people joy. Knowing that you were part of that process is just amazing.

I've been volunteering for nine years now. I'm often asked about the history of the dogs that we've rescued or fostered. Honestly, most of the time I can't remember. I'm focused on helping the dog through its journey toward a forever home; toward a relaxed, non-anxious being; toward love. Their journeys began long before they came into rescue, and my goal is to find the correct path for each individual dog. Our priority is placing dogs with the best people, not people with the best dogs. The dogs' safety and happiness come first, which is why they always thrive in their new homes.

I hope my volunteering sets an example for my family and friends about helping to better our community. Both my kids grew up with lots of dogs in the house and watched so many of those dogs find new families. They helped train them and walk them and have always been very involved in the adoption process. I always wanted to teach my kids to be good people and to contribute to society, so it's very rewarding that way. My son's grown up now and living on his own, and it's so nice to see he's pursued volunteer work—not with my encouragement, but simply because he wanted to. I'm so happy about that.

VOLUNTEER Tierney Crocker

DOG Sammy

RESCUE GROUP Berkshire Humane Society (Pittsfield, Massachusetts)

I just graduated from Berkshire Community College (BCC), where we all had to do service learning projects. We'd spend fifteen hours volunteering with a nonprofit organization and get class credit. I took environmental science at BCC, so I thought volunteering here would be a good fit. To be honest, at first I was not into volunteering by any means. I just saw it as something I had to do to pass a class. Then fifteen hours turned into many, many more, and I ended up volunteering for a few months. An hour a day in the afternoon is so nice. You just go for a walk, get some exercise, and play with the dogs. How can you walk into a room of dogs and not be happy?

The first day I came in, I thought, *These dogs have it made!* I was used to seeing sad shelter dogs looking pathetic on those TV commercials, but I walked in and saw all these happy shelter dogs with blankets and toys and a yard to play in. I quickly realized that shelters aren't depressing at all, but places full of happy dogs.

Most people assume that because someone didn't want their dog, it must not be a good dog, but there are so many different reasons why dogs end up in the shelter. Maybe someone has kids and the dog is too big, or the person has allergies. Whatever the reason, it has nothing to do with the dog—it has to do with what the people are going through.

Watching a dog finally get adopted makes me happy. I know that they're not going to be sleeping alone in a kennel by themselves anymore. I know they've got a family, and a yard to play in, and people who will be there for them. There are no bad dogs here.

VOLUNTEER Connor Cook

DOG Mosey

RESCUE GROUP BADRAP (Oakland, California)

For the past six years, I've had the Sunday morning volunteer shift at BADRAP. I call it my "Sunday morning service." I get up early and leave my dog and wife asleep in bed. When I get up to the BADRAP barn, it's quiet and beautiful. I feel secure up there. The dogs are having a good time, and I'm having a good time with them. I believe that being with the dogs is like a meditation class. They teach me to simply be in the moment. It's pure joy watching them play, and it's so sweet when the dogs incorporate me into it. I struggle with my own anxieties on a daily basis, but when I'm up there, I feel safe and secure and happy. That's better than any therapy for me.

Dogs don't need much and they don't ask for much, but they give back one hundred times what they get—even when people have been terrible to them. A lot of the dogs that we rescue come from horrible situations, and you wouldn't even know it by the way they act, the way they treat people. It's like they're able to simply move past those torturous experiences once they realize they're finally safe.

Volunteering is teaching me to not worry about so many things. The dogs help me reprioritize what really matters: connecting with people, with dogs, and being in the moment. When I'm up at the barn, I give myself permission to just focus on what I'm doing, because the dogs demand that. I feel fully engaged with the animals because they are fully engaged with me. There's a mutual caretaking that happens. It's not a one-sided relationship. If we pay attention to what the dogs give us versus what we give them, we're really getting the good end of this deal.

VOLUNTEER Lara Kelly

DOG Jacie

RESCUE GROUP Animal Care and Control Team Philly
(Philadelphia, Pennsylvania)

I started volunteering about six years ago after I heard a story on social media about a dog who was making himself sick. The dog was so well house-trained that when he was surrendered to the shelter, he refused to pee in his crate. Dogs at that shelter were only getting out every four to five days. I figured that being house-trained is something we humans taught these dogs, so it's our fault that this dog was making himself sick. It's our fault that he can't get outside except for every four to five days. I figured I could do something about that, and that was the beginning of my volunteering.

I feel an obligation to the animals because they did nothing wrong to end up here. It's not jail. They are here because of circumstance, timing, and bad luck.

Even though I'll leave the shelter and know that I could have spent another six hours here, I leave with a very full heart. I come three days a week when I can, and sometimes I bring the family on the weekend. My daughter just turned ten, and she's been coming here ever since she was little. I think it's important for kids to realize how it all works.

When I started volunteering, it felt the same way it does now—completely overwhelming. I live about fifteen minutes away from the shelter, and every time I hit a certain point in the road, I get knots in my stomach. Some days are great, but it's always the worst place on earth. As hard as volunteering is, I've made some really great friends here whom I know I'll be friends with for the rest of my life. We've found that we have much more in common than the dogs. But while there are dogs here, I will keep coming.

VOLUNTEERS Jean and Vern Simpson

DOG Fletcher

RESCUE GROUP Big Fluffy Dog Rescue (Nashville, Tennessee)

Jean: We never volunteered together before Big Fluffy, but we've had dogs all our lives. One day we were looking for a schnauzer—we'd always had schnauzers or Brittanys. We were on vacation, and one of the Big Fluffy volunteers called and said they had a dog that looked very much like our Brittany that had died. She said, "I'm going to send you the picture." We were in Missouri at the time, but we stopped and immediately filled out the application to foster that dog over the phone.

Vern: I love companionship, and these dogs don't have a good chance. If we don't help them, they won't have a good outcome.

Jean: We've fostered sixteen dogs so far. The longest we had one was five weeks. We almost "failed" with him. I cried horribly when we put him back on transport.

Vern: It was a sheltie.

Jean: Right, it was a sheltie. We had four Great Pyrenees puppies once, and that was a real treat. We're not really puppy people.

Vern: Our last dog was a rescue.

Jean: Yes, our last Brittany was a rescue. These dogs would die were it not for volunteers, so we know we're making a difference. Volunteering has made a big difference with my grandchildren, too. I have a three-year-old grandson who lives in Franklin, Tennessee. Back in the winter he stayed with us for a while. We'd take him to the John Deere dealer every two or three days. People would constantly come up to us and say, "What a beautiful dog you have." I would say, "He's a rescue from Big Fluffy." One day the manager came up to me and said, "What a beautiful dog you have." My grandson said, "He's a rescue from Big Fluffy." That says it all.

VOLUNTEER Ron Dischert

DOG Pollydoodle

RESCUE GROUP Austin Animal Services (Austin, Texas)

I was recovering from neck surgery a couple years back, and while I was walking at our Town Lake trail one day, I saw people from the shelter walking dogs. I thought, *Why don't I do that?* And that's really how I got started. I've been volunteering for about seven years now.

I do a lot of different things at the shelter, but my main focus is with the Hard Luck Hounds program. We work with the dogs that are "adoption challenged": the unpopular breeds, the deaf or blind dogs, dogs with correctable behavioral issues, etc.

I am so thrilled when a dog gets adopted or goes into a foster home. I get teary-eyed, as you can see. I mean, there have been setbacks—we had one dog come back, owner-surrendered, about a week ago. But I've already got a champion lined up for that dog. We're going to start marketing her and get her out of here again.

Volunteering is great exercise. I clocked over nine miles yesterday on my Fitbit. Yesterday was only about a five- or six-hour day, but Monday I did a ten-and-a-half-hour day. I drove way, way down south to check up on one of our Hard Luck Hounds, just to make sure that the adopters aren't having issues. We like to see the animal in their home setting to assess how they're doing. The person who started this program went back to work full-time, so he asked me to step in and take it over. I'm retired, I'm type A, I love dogs, and I love people. I'm just very motivated by this work—it's amazing and rewarding.

VOLUNTEER Eric Martinez

DOG Junior

RESCUE GROUP El Paso Animal Services (El Paso, Texas)

After you find an animal a home, it's like a bit of a high. It's hard knowing that we can't save them all, but then again, it's not our fault or the shelter's fault. A lot of people are breeding dogs or think they can have pets even though they really can't. Those people end up coming here to surrender their dogs, and someone's got to be here for them.

Volunteering is relaxing. There's a lot of other stuff I could be doing with my time, but this is really positive. We take the animals out for walks and train some of them. When visitors come in, we help them find their next family member. I don't know how most people treat their dogs, but I treat them like family members—like my kids.

These dogs depend on us, and they amaze me sometimes. You'll see the meanest-looking dog in there be so humble. You'll see little Chihuahuas with so much energy. That's one of the things we'll show people when they come in looking for dogs. We'll tell them, "This dog can do this! This dog can do that!" That way they know it's not just going to be a pet to take care of; it's going to be something to really enjoy.

Just yesterday there was a couple in here looking to adopt a dog, and they kept asking me, "Well, can I see this one? Can I see that one?" Sometimes you'll wonder, are they going to adopt or not? But in the end they do, so it's all worth it. People laugh at me, but when I put an animal back in its cage, I say, "You're going home, buddy!" Even though they don't understand what I'm saying, they know that I've got their back.

When I was living in Florida, my husband and I would go look at the dogs at the shelter. I'd always come out weeping. I knew there was a Humane Society in the Berkshires, and when we moved up here, I thought, *You know, crying isn't helping. Spending time with them, doing things with them—that's going to help the animals.* The opportunity was finally there to volunteer, and I just told myself, "Get over it." I sniffled my way through my first shift at the shelter, and then it got better, and it continued getting better every time. Eleven years later I'm still here.

I've got my own animals at home, but nothing beats helping these shelter dogs find a home. Instead of looking at these dogs and thinking, *Who could give this animal up?* I realized that being at the shelter was actually another chance for them to find a great home. Volunteering gives me so much satisfaction, and it's an opportunity to love the animals and get love in return.

It's so rewarding when they finally go home. It's kind of like graduation. There was a dog that had been here over a year, and one Thursday night it was evident that she was going home. A family had come in and looked at her several times. The shelter closes at eight, and all the volunteers were here, waiting in the lobby until that family finally walked out with that dog. We all clapped and watched as they signed the adoption papers and saw her off.

I'm so glad I got over the sniffles and decided to do this. You really get to be part of such a great community. It's really given me something to focus on outside of myself. It's changed my life.

VOLUNTEER Paige Gruda

DOG Joey

RESCUE GROUP McKinley County Humane Society (Gallup, New Mexico)

I got started volunteering two or three years ago, when I was seventeen. My mom saw an ad in the newspaper saying that the shelter needed more foster families, and she thought we would give it a try.

Ever since then we've been fostering animals and helping these shelter animals get placed into rescues out of state. They've just got a higher chance at adoption at a bigger shelter, in a bigger city. My mom's the one who transports all the animals out. Every week she'll drive a van full of animals to the next city, sometimes farther.

I don't know how many animals my mom and I have saved over the years—I've lost count. It's somewhere in the hundreds, or maybe more. I've always loved animals, since I was little. Because we're a high-kill shelter, it makes me really happy when I know I've saved an animal's life just by doing what I love to do.

VOLUNTEER Kris Gruda

DOG Blanca

RESCUE GROUP McKinley County Humane Society (Gallup, New Mexico)

I've always loved animals, and one day I saw in the paper that they needed fosters, so I decided to start fostering. I was afraid I'd get stuck with the animals because there aren't a lot of homes or families around here looking to adopt a pet. However, once I learned that a lot of our animals get transported to other rescues and shelters, I decided to go ahead and foster, since there was a place for the animals to go to eventually. The need is just so great that once you get started, I don't feel like you can stop. You've just got to keep helping the animals. If you don't, there's one less person helping.

I'm the transport coordinator at McKinley, and I'm also a foster. We have such a huge overpopulation of animals here. Not many people come into the shelter to adopt a pet, because you can just as easily pick up one on the side of the road. Often, too, their own dogs are having puppies and they can just take one of those. So getting our shelter animals out of the area is crucial to saving their lives and finding them homes.

Every time a van full of animals leaves, I feel like I really accomplished something. Those lives might not have continued if that transport hadn't happened, so it's a good feeling. I'll usually just do the shorter transport drives up to Sedona or Flagstaff, because I have a full-time job. It gets to be a lot sometimes. Too much, sometimes. But I hang in there. If I don't do it, I'm not sure anybody else will. And if I stop, more dogs are probably not going to make it out.

VOLUNTEERS Bob and Erica Klevay

DOG Tammy and Charlie

RESCUE GROUP Montgomery Humane Society (Montgomery, Alabama)

Erica: We're here together every Sunday pretty faithfully. We walk the big dogs. They are harder to walk, so they weren't being walked as much as the small dogs.

Bob: We just kind of stuck with it.

Erica: Part of the reason why we're regular volunteers is because it's part of our schedule. On Sunday we come to the shelter, and then we go grocery shopping and do the laundry.

Bob: Yeah. It's not a very romantic thing, but it's so scheduled now that it would seem weird to *not* be doing it. Volunteering is hard. Sometimes I think people try to take on too much and end up dropping out because they don't find their place in the shelter. But if you find that one spot and persist at it . . .

Erica: . . . it can be really rewarding. I don't think we'd have come back every Sunday for three years if we didn't feel that it was rewarding. I know more dogs in Montgomery than people, because we walk them every Sunday. So, you know, if we miss a week I wonder how . . .

Bob: . . . they're doing. Volunteering gives us extra time to do something together. When one of us doesn't want to go, the other one will usually drag us in. And let's be honest, it's usually you trying to get me to do stuff on Sundays.

Erica: No matter what I do for the rest of my life, every Sunday the dogs have a better time because I came and walked them. That is an important thing to me. It feels really good.

VOLUNTEERS Madeleine Faust and her son Simon Smith

DOG Penny

RESCUE GROUP Used Dogs Rescue (New Orleans, Louisiana)

Madeleine: One day this stray pit bull found me. I had no idea what to do with her. I got on the Internet and looked up pit bull rescues. I called the place that bills itself as a pit bull rescue, and they said, "Oh, we don't take in strays. We're strictly educational." Then I found [the director of Used Dogs] Madalin's number, and I gave her a call. She said, "Let me come over and meet this dog." She came over at nine thirty p.m. on a work night, gave the dog a temperament test, and said, "I'll help you find a home if you can keep the dog for a while." Madalin impressed me so much that night that we all started volunteering for Used Dogs.

Simon: I was ten or eleven when I started. One day my mom said, "Do you want to come volunteer with us this Saturday?" and I said, "Why not?"

Madeleine: My older son volunteers, too. Every Saturday he would help hose the kennels down, walk the dogs, and do just about everything else. I don't have time to save all the homeless dogs out there because I have to raise my kids, so I'm going to help Madalin do it.

Simon: It's kind of something to do to keep your mind clear. It's like a catharsis at the end of the day. You get a cleansing feeling after you work with the dogs.

Madeleine: It is also a way to spend time together. When the kids started becoming teenagers, you know, they didn't want to hang around with their mom. It's nice to have them with me when I volunteer.

I believe that fostering care for your fellow creatures is important. I think dogs are probably the noblest creatures in the world. When I die and come back as a dog, I sure as hell hope someone like Madalin finds me.

VOLUNTEER Will McKinney

DOG Brandy

RESCUE GROUP Austin Animal Services (Austin, Texas)

I have always liked dogs and decided that I wanted to help enrich their lives. I've been volunteering for a year and two months.

When I'm here, I walk them and I do a little bit of training, too. Without the volunteers the dogs would be stuck in their kennels all day, so I like to give them some time outside to play fetch in the yard.

If I'm in a bad mood, oftentimes being here puts me in a better mood, believe it or not. It takes me outside of myself. I'm usually in my head, thinking about my own problems. Coming out here and playing with the dogs takes me away from worrying about myself. I guess that's why I'm happier when I'm here—I only think about the good that I'm doing for the dogs and try to block out the rest.

The dogs only get out once or twice a day. Some visitors find it hard to see them in their kennels because it's just so different from a home environment. And it's hard for me, too, especially if I leave the shelter before a lot of dogs have had their first walk of the day. But you know, some of these dogs are really people oriented, like Brandy. She needs this love. I've noticed that the dogs who are the most rambunctious tend to love people the most. It's just so hard for them to see people walk by and not take them out of the kennel. I think all dogs need to get out and do what dogs do: sniff the ground, bark, all that good stuff. The kennels here are a pretty good size, but there's no substitute for getting out in the grass and running around and getting exercise. It's good for them, and it's good for me.

VOLUNTEER Cody Roberson

DOG Corin

RESCUE GROUP Big Fluffy Dog Rescue (Nashville, Tennessee)

When I first moved to Tennessee, I had a full-time job at a vet's office, and our office would help take care of some of the Big Fluffy dogs. A friend of mine worked here at the rescue, so I decided to start volunteering. I was basically working eighty hours a week between my real job and the rescue, but I got to see the dogs that I helped at the vet's office get adopted. That's why I stuck around. After a while Big Fluffy offered me a paid position, so I quit my full-time job.

Everyone thought I was crazy. But I took the job because I couldn't see myself doing anything else. I would dream about dogs at night, dream about all the rescues that we worked with.

We grow as people by being able to see how mistreated these dogs were and then getting to see them become beloved pets in someone's home. We get to tell people what we do and raise public awareness. Big Fluffy Dog Rescue is one of the largest dog rescues in the area, and we save a lot of dogs.

I remember my first time pulling a dog from a shelter. It was a little bitty white-and-brown dog. This dog was super scared and really timid. She wouldn't let a lot of people get close to her, but we worked with her for a couple months and then she got adopted. I met her a year later, after being in her adoptive home in Connecticut. It was the greatest feeling in the world. You think, *I saved that dog's life. I was there for that dog when no one else was, and I was able to get it into a home and give it a second chance.*

VOLUNTEER Donna Reynolds, director

DOG Chiquita

RESCUE GROUP BADRAP (Oakland, California)

During the late 1990s pit bulls were facing a crisis in the San Francisco Bay Area, and nobody was doing anything about it. So we said, "Let's see if we can make a little bit of a difference." We pulled our first pit bull, Sally, from Berkeley Animal Care Services before BADRAP had even started. We thought it shouldn't be too terribly hard to find her a home.

It was horrific. Nobody would give her the time of day. We found other independent pit bull rescuers via the Internet in Oakland and came up with a plan.

Tim and I had never rescued a pit bull. I was afraid to make a mistake. It was my own fear that held me back. But when I saw Sally at the shelter, she just got to me. She seemed like she was very happy to see me, and also like she was grieving for her former life. I understood what she was experiencing in that moment, and I wanted to change that for her. I let go of my fear and said, "Let's go, let's get out of here." And that's how BADRAP started years ago.

Everybody comes to the rescue world looking to fill different voids. Some people want companionship, some want to be alone with an animal and away from people, and some want to improve their dog-handling skills. These animals bring out the best in us, and they want us to be ourselves. We get to shed some of our masks and simply be with them. That makes us better people, better humans.

Tim and I both came from an art background, so we consider this work to be an art project of a sort. Taking something that people don't see any value in and turning that into something beautiful. Whether I'm doing it with an animal or with an art piece, it's still the same desire to help people to see beauty.

Chiquita Finds a Home

Chiquita had a hard time finding her forever family. She stayed at the BADRAP barn for months and months and was frequently passed over for younger dogs.

The scars from her years in the dogfighting ring scared people away, even though she was a joyful dog. It took a very special, loving, and nonjudgmental person to see through that darkness and embrace the beauty inside Chiquita. Finally, a match was made when BAD-RAP's director made a very special introduction to a woman named Eliza Wheeler. This is Eliza's story:

I had gone through a really hard time prior to getting Chiquita, and she's not at all who I was looking for at the time. I was trying to find a replacement for my old dog. I lost him after my partner and I split up, and I was so heartbroken that I wanted to get a dog just like him.

Chiquita was the exact opposite, but she is just so forgiving, present, and confident even though she's been through so much awful stuff. In the end I guess that's exactly who I needed. She reminded me that sometimes we just go through hard stuff and that we're still okay; it's in the past. We're here now. And that's exactly how she is. So, really, she became the perfect dog for what I needed.

We don't know the whole story of her past, but we have the clues from her body. She was one of nine dogs that were rescued from a dogfighting ring in the South. Those dogs were then brought into BADRAP's program. She has a lot of physical scars. She has a bad burn on her back, her front leg was broken and never healed right, and she's missing most of her teeth. When I first got her, I couldn't help but see all of that, all of the time. Sometimes it would make me cry just looking at her. But now I never think about it because I don't think Chiquita thinks about it. She is just a dog. She has a whole new world now. She has friends and toys and lot of dog beds and gets fancy bones from the butcher. She is so happy, and she lives in the moment. In that sense she's become my teacher. That's what she brought into my life. That's what I needed when I got her—somebody to remind me to just be in the moment and let go of stuff that happened in the past. What better teacher than a dog?

There really are people in the world who believe that a dog like Chiquita is unfit to live in society. It never occurred to me that she couldn't be given a chance.

To me she's just a dog. At first there's a lot of attachment to her traumatic backstory, because it's horrific and she bears those scars. At first it's hard to not think of her as a victim. But gradually you see that she's just a dog. She's just a happy, forgiving little creature that lives in this moment, and I've really never met a dog like her.

VOLUNTEERS Heidi Herrera, Kristina Madden, Jacqueline Madden, and Amanda Herrera

DOGS Shale and Max

RESCUE GROUP El Paso Animal Services (El Paso, Texas)

Heidi: I was working for the El Paso Police Department. One day I got an e-mail saying that they needed volunteers here at the shelter. I thought, *Yeah, that's definitely something I want to do.*

Jacqueline: When the shelter opened, the euthanasia rate was 80 percent. We're down to 60 percent only a year later, which is amazing. It's getting much better, thanks to the VIP program, in which volunteers spend a lot of one-on-one time with dogs that are deemed highly adoptable. It really helps them succeed.

Kristina: Any time we get a dog adopted, we'll text each other and say, "I just got this dog adopted!" It makes your whole day better.

Jacqueline: You're literally saving that dog's life on that day.

Heidi: I know that each of us have had that day. You have been working so hard to get this one dog adopted, and then you have to see it get walked the green mile. Not everyone can say that they make a difference in the world, but I can.

Kristina: We get asked all the time, "How can you work there?" I always say, "Because somebody has to!" If there's no one here, more dogs will be put to sleep.

Amanda: And who would play with them?

Kristina: Right.

Amanda: Who's going to love those dogs? Who's going to hug them and pet them and play with them if no one volunteers?

Jacqueline: If I can make that dog's day better for ten minutes, that was ten minutes it wasn't terrified, or ten minutes it wasn't upset. That's why I show up.

VOLUNTEER Nicole Butler

DOGS Professor Quiggins, Max, and Festus

RESCUE GROUP Big Fluffy Dog Rescue (Nashville, Tennessee)

About a year and a half ago, I saw a Facebook post saying that Big Fluffy needed someone to foster a mom and her six puppies. I thought, *Can I really do this? Well, I'm single. Sure I can!* So I went ahead and responded.

After that the foster coordinator hooked me up with two senior dogs that were in a really bad way. I put my all into fostering those dogs, but I didn't expect to see such a huge transformation. They finally went to a wonderful forever home, and I'm still in touch with the adopters—we're friends now.

From there I was hooked. I was heartbroken when those foster dogs left, so Big Fluffy brought me another dog to foster. He was my first orthopedic case. Now I've become the orthopedic specialist foster.

I've fostered thirty-five dogs in the past fifteen months. I had a litter of nine puppies. That was insane. I had an amputee and another orthopedic dog at the same time. That was a bit much. But you know, live and learn.

I always want the worst of the worst. Those are the ones I want to rehab and fix. Partly it's selfish, to see that huge transformation. It makes you feel so good to see the dog go from scared, timid, unsure, and in pain to happy and thriving.

It's been so important to teach my kids how helping animals is just as important as helping people. I think they're getting it. My kids are three and six. Do you know what the littlest one told me that she wanted to do to the man that put these scars on this dog? I won't repeat it, but it involved a Zippo lighter. They definitely are going to be the protectors of those that can't protect themselves—on four legs or two.

VOLUNTEER Katie Hemphill

DOG George

RESCUE GROUP Used Dogs Rescue (New Orleans, Louisiana)

I lost a friend to suicide in 2012, and it really changed me. I started seeing things differently, seeing things that I never used to see before. Then Hurricane Isaac happened, and I felt like I needed to reach out. It was a coincidence that I found this great group. I agree with so many of Madalin's philosophies, and we all get along so well. I could never do what she does, but if I did, I'd do it exactly the same way.

I've stuck with this group, and I love it. I've been volunteering for a little over three years now. I come here once a week on the weekend, and I also do adoption events. I walk the dogs, do some training with them, and clean some kennels.

There are so many things to be sad about in life. It's hard enough making other people happy, much less yourself. But it takes so little to make these dogs happy—knowing that I can do one little thing is an incredible feeling. Who wouldn't want to go somewhere every week where the little thing makes such a positive impact? It just makes you feel good. I can take a dog for a walk, clean them, or pet them, and all of a sudden the dogs are happy and I'm happy. Whenever things feel complicated, this is always something I come back to.

VOLUNTEER Jenna and Gus Turk

DOG McCoy

RESCUE GROUP Big Fluffy Dog Rescue (Nashville, Tennessee)

I first found Big Fluffy because I was looking to adopt a dog, a particular dog, and someone recommended Big Fluffy. I started following them on Facebook, and I kept seeing all these pleas for foster volunteers. Finally, one day, I said, "You know, it doesn't cost me anything. There's no downside for me." So I started fostering. Now I'm kind of the puppy lady. I'm really set up for small puppies, the smaller the better. Our last foster was a mama and her six newborns. They came home to us the day she had them, so we got to raise six babies. It was awesome.

I have three kids, ages thirteen, ten, and three. Fostering for Big Fluffy is teaching them responsibility. My older boys do a lot of the cleaning. When there are kennels that need to be cleaned, they get that, and they have to clean up the yard. If they can, they go with me to vet appointments to help, especially if I have multiple dogs. It's taught them compassion. Especially the little one. He loves these dogs. He just loves on them, and he protects them, and he will tell people, "This is my dog, and you have to be gentle." So it's teaching them about doing good and caring for someone or something else without getting anything in return.

I'm trying to just put some good out into the world. I've always been an animal lover. I know that in reality we can't save them all. However, it makes me feel good to know that I've played a part in saving one animal at a time.

VOLUNTEER Madalin Bernard, director

DOG Penny

RESCUE GROUP Used Dogs Rescue (New Orleans, Louisiana)

A few months after I moved back here, I was walking over by the river and saw a dog coming around the corner. It looked like a brown dog, but as it got closer, I realized it was actually an overbred white pit bull that was covered in fleas. She walked up to me and collapsed. I spent three hours getting the fleas off of her and then took her everywhere trying to get her help. I named her Sarah. Everyone told me she was vicious and that she'd eat my face off because she was a pit bull, but my instinct told me that wasn't true. I nursed Sarah back to health, and the world was a better place for all the love that she gave. There's an old saying: "Be careful what you end up doing, because you'll end up doing it." I rescued that dog, and then there was another one, and there's never been a shortage of dogs since.

After Hurricane Katrina I continued rescuing dogs. I was discovering a lot about myself in the process. I do well in hurricanes. When it's really clear what needs to be done, I'm like Superwoman. When times are easy, I fret about what to do. I don't half-ass things, so I decided to stay in New Orleans after the hurricane. I certainly wasn't going to half-ass animal rescue.

I get so many calls from people who want to start their own rescue groups. I always tell them: The first thing you need to do is volunteer. I never really put it into words, but what happened with Sarah changed my life.

I actually feel like I've gotten more from the dogs than I've ever given to them. In this life I found patience and empathy that I never thought I had. Even though it's a real struggle, I'll always believe that there's value in doing this work.

VOLUNTEER Juan Mora

DOG Name Unknown

RESCUE GROUP El Paso Animal Services (El Paso, Texas)

I'm here to help these guys find a new home, because everybody needs a good home. I'm trying to make people understand that these dogs are not aggressive. A lot of people come here to get Chihuahuas, and sometimes I make them leave with a German shepherd. I tell them, "Let the dog come to you. If it comes to you, try to give it a home." As long as they take a dog or any animal from here, it makes me feel better. I hear all the stories about how fighting dogs get emotionally shut down, but it's not the dog's fault. It's the owner's fault, and that's why I always meet the adopters first. If they're nice, I'll help them out. I do everything for these dogs, just to get them out of here. I volunteer because I love dogs and I want to be around them.

I came here initially with my stepdaughter. She's five years old. My little Sofia loves cats, so we got her a shelter cat. His name is Tony. When we came here, I went to the back and saw all the dogs. The volunteers told me about how so many of them get put down. Right then I asked if I could volunteer, and I just kept coming in. I'm going to keep on coming in even if I go back to work.

I sleep better knowing that these dogs are going to a good home. I've been incarcerated, and I know that being locked up does not feel good. You need to be out there; you need to have your freedom to have a good life. And these animals deserve it. That's why I volunteer.

VOLUNTEER Jim Richardson

DOG Amelia

RESCUE GROUP The Little Guild of Saint Francis
(West Cornwall, Connecticut)

This was one of the things that I thought I would enjoy doing when I retired. It gives me a chance to give back to animals that don't get as much good luck in the world as they deserve. I like the attitude of the Little Guild. They don't give up on a dog just because she may be hard to place.

We had a dog that was here the whole first two years that I was volunteering. Josie was a great little dog, but she didn't show well when people would look at her. She'd jump up and down in her kennel, because she wanted to get out. She didn't always give the best impression, but Little Guild stuck with her and finally found a home for her that worked. That's one of the things that I like about them. They really try to match the personality of the dog or cat with the personality of the individual adopter or family.

Why would you buy a purebred dog when you can get a perfectly great rescue dog at the shelter and give it a second chance? This gal's a great little dog, but for whatever reason, black dogs are always harder to adopt out. People are more in tune with dogs like yellow Labs or huskies because they see more of them, but there are a lot of other good dogs, too.

I come down Wednesday morning and spend three or four hours just walking with the dogs alone in the woods. And to me that's great. I enjoy being in the woods, and I don't mind being alone. I talk to the dogs, and they're always happy to see me. It's a rewarding experience. These guys, even when they're hurting, always seem to be appreciative of the time you're spending with them.

VOLUNTEER Amberly Crawford

DOG Maude

RESCUE GROUP Montgomery Humane Society (Montgomery, Alabama)

I joined a great big church three years ago called TAG, which stands for That Animal Group. It's somewhat like a rescue group. That's where I met Cindy Chapman, our volunteer coordinator. She was asking for volunteers for an upcoming adoption event, so I decided to help her out. Because I wasn't an official volunteer, I had to go through volunteer orientation training. I was intimidated at first because I didn't want to mess up. My first volunteer experience was going on a field trip to PetSmart with Ray, a quiet and shy dog. I call myself quiet and shy sometimes, so we were a perfect match. But Ray wasn't getting excited when people came by during the event, so he got overlooked. That's when I decided to keep coming back to the shelter to help him get adopted, and I've been coming here ever since.

The animals need a voice. They can't speak for themselves. I come and volunteer to help them. I know anything I do at the shelter helps them get adopted, from cleaning the cages to sorting newspaper, from giving them water to working on fund-raisers.

I usually come in from two to five every Saturday afternoon. I also help out with special events, and I sort newspapers at home and bring them in. People know that I'm a volunteer here, so they'll give me their shredded paper for the dog's crates. Sometimes they'll give me food if their cat or dog doesn't like a food. They know I can bring it to the shelter. They think I'm an expert because I volunteer here, which is kind of neat. At the end of the day, I know I did a good job, that I made a difference for the animals, and that I am a voice for the shelter.

VOLUNTEER Allegra Haldeman

DOG Name Unknown

RESCUE GROUP Animal Care and Control Team Philly
(Philadelphia, Pennsylvania)

I was a social worker for a multiple sclerosis association. Everything was going great in my life, so I decided it was time to get a dog. I adopted a three-legged Chihuahua from a rescue that pulled him from this very shelter, actually. I had him for a little while, and then I started to think about all the people who had helped him on his journey. Before I adopted him, he had gone through three different foster homes and was returned twice. I was just so impressed with that entire process and all the people who cared for him. That's when I decided that I wanted to give back to the shelter system. I applied here when the community programs manager position opened up. There's a sense of urgency, and the employees and volunteers here work extremely hard to get animals out.

It was my goal to make a bigger impact. I really like working with people. That's why I've always been involved with volunteers and fosters. I get to do all the happy, people-related tasks here. My ultimate goal is to do something more community based, where I'm helping the local community keep their pets. People in the community love their animals, and I'm sure their animals love them. Sometimes people hit rough patches. If they could just get a little bit of support, everyone would be better off and fewer people would be forced to surrender their dogs to the shelter.

It's rough. Some days are harder than others. It's kind of like a rush. You're constantly fighting and trying to beat the odds. But when you're driving home and thinking about your day, you're like, "Holy crap! We accomplished so much in a single day!" You drive home knowing you can relax and have a good night, knowing that you did the best that you could.

VOLUNTEERS Amy and Alexis Marrufo

DOG Delilah

RESCUE GROUP El Paso Animal Services (El Paso, Texas)

Alexis: We recently had a lot of problems with money, which was really hard because we weren't able to give our dogs everything they needed. We had to come to the shelter and surrender them, and we were devastated. They were our babies. I guess we started volunteering in order to help us heal.

Amy: We didn't want to drag them down with us. We actually found out about the volunteer program when we surrendered them here, so volunteering let us keep track of our dogs and make sure they got adopted—and they did within a week. We were so thankful that someone took them in that we decided to try to pass that good deed on to another shelter dog. Now, apparently, we can't get away.

Alexis: Looking into these dogs' eyes is looking into our own dogs' eyes. You know that they're going to have a new life. You're not going to give up on them. They deserve a lot better than being stuck in here.

Amy: It used to be a competition. We'd see how many dogs we could get adopted in one day—I think our max is thirteen.
Yeah, we got thirteen adopted in one day.

Alexis: It was amazing.
I think we have the highest rank here, huh?

Amy: They call us the sibling team. We're five years apart, so we have our differences. But when it comes to this . . .

VOLUNTEER Wayne Douglas

DOG Whopper

RESCUE GROUP The Little Guild of Saint Francis
(West Cornwall, Connecticut)

I retired from the power company four years ago and saw an ad on the public access channel about the Little Guild. I said, "I'll walk a dog!" They said, "Oh, we've got just the dog for you." He was a little rough around the edges, but he was a good dog.

I started coming back every day to work with him. Then I went to another dog, then two dogs, and it just turned into what it was. Now I come down five to seven days a week for two hours. I walk them, and I also try to train them a little bit out in the field. Every dog does something different. Some of them like to hunt. Some of them don't even want to go for a walk. They just want to sit down, which is sad. They just want comfort. I do the same thing in Florida when I go down there for a couple of months each year. I go to the local city shelter, and they're in the same situation as here—they have no help, no money. Same thing, different state, same state of mind.

The shelters need the help, and it feels good to me to be paying my penance. You can tell that some of the animals have been abused. Some of them come around in a month, some in just two or three days. It can take a lot of time for them to get readjusted.

I couldn't do what the staff do. Volunteering is easy. Taking the dogs for a walk, teaching them to sit and roll over—that's a lot easier than cleaning kennels and running the shelter. Volunteering's like having grandchildren. You get to play with them; then it's "See ya later!"

VOLUNTEER Linda Chute

DOG Sheila

RESCUE GROUP Downey Animal Care Center (Los Angeles, California)

I'm the pit bull advocate here, because they're the underdog. I tell everyone, "You shouldn't judge them until you meet them, because they're an amazing breed." Still, they are the hardest dogs to get out of the shelter. I want to be there for all the dogs, even the ones who I know won't make it out. They deserve at least that much.

I think I get more from the dogs than they get from me. When new volunteers come in, I tell them that I cry every time I leave the shelter. I cry when they get adopted, when they get rescued, and when they get euthanized. But I always get something back from these dogs, and then I pay it forward to the next dog. If I lose a dog, I think, *I'm going to save another dog in their name.* That's what you have to do. Even if we can't save them all, we should at least be there for them and let them know we love them before they leave the shelter.

Every dog that comes through the shelter system is simply looking for someone to love them, and not everyone understands that. A lot people think it's too difficult to come into the shelter, but you just may find that one dog that's going to change your whole life. You have to believe in these dogs. That's what it's all about. They make you happy, and they don't expect anything from you in return.

It's not always a happy ending, but you have to give what you can. If my only job for the whole day at the shelter is to sit and love on the dogs, to hold them and tell them I love them before they are euthanized, then I feel like I did something for them. I'm not going to desert them; I'm going to stay there with them and I'll be there to the end, whatever the outcome is. I'll be there.

VOLUNTEER Sarah Tames

DOG Tigger

RESCUE GROUP The Little Guild of Saint Francis
(West Cornwall, Connecticut)

I taught English at a private boarding school for twenty-eight years. For me, teaching is so much about being empathetic and available, trying to figure out what blocks a student might be having. That's the same approach I take with animals, especially animals in this situation. They are stressed in their kennels. Some of them were dumped here, some of them had people and then their people died, so they're confused. There's a lot that is hard for these animals, and if we can help them be more comfortable, they will be more easily adoptable.

I think that working with animals requires a lot of empathy. That can be hard, too, because sometimes it's heartbreaking. I have such awe for the staff people who work so hard with these animals. There are times when an animal comes to the shelter with an illness that we didn't know about. That can be really heartbreaking, because some of those dogs have to get put down. It's a very difficult choice. But the flip side is fabulous. Everybody here is so happy the day a dog is adopted—it's like a celebration. Everybody comes out to say goodbye to the dog, and some adopters are very good about coming back and bringing their dogs back to visit, which we all love.

I believe there's a sense of responsibility to this, too. I think that the reason shelters exist is because we human beings have done a pretty lousy job caring for our animals. We've created this problem, and it's awful. Not everyone can come walk dogs, but those who can't physically volunteer can give money. It can be five dollars. It can be stopping at the grocery store and picking up some cans of food. People don't have to do a lot to make a difference. I think we should all do that.

VOLUNTEER Lennie Hammit

DOG Svetta

RESCUE GROUP McKinley County Humane Society (Gallup, New Mexico)

I had to complete some community service hours in 2012. I was only supposed to volunteer for five hours each day, but I started staying later and later; even when it's time to go, there's still work that needs to be done. I stayed at the shelter until they closed. Now I'm here late each night doing second feedings for the youngest animals, keeping them on a schedule and bathing them.

The animals all deserve to be loved. Even spending some time sitting with them like this makes them so happy. They need the attention. What really makes me upset is when people get puppies this small and then abandon them when they grow up. That's just really, really sad because they didn't do anything wrong.

I have a book where I keep track of every animal coming in and out of the shelter. It's just something that I wanted to be responsible for. It's a lot of work, but when they're healthy and have gotten their vaccinations, the animals can get on a rescue transport to Arizona or Colorado. That's what makes me happy.

Now, every second week of the month, some of us from the shelter will go to the Arts Crawl and hand out brochures about spay/neuter services. We'll take a couple of these guys with us to see if we can adopt them out. We really encourage people to spay and neuter their pets. A lot of animals get abandoned that way—they just keep populating, and that's why we've got strays everywhere. My mission is to take care of these guys and speak for them, because they don't have a voice.

VOLUNTEER Jeremiah Herman

DOG Picasso

RESCUE GROUP Muttville Senior Dog Rescue (San Francisco, California)

I completed a school internship volunteering at Muttville, and it was so awesome being there that I couldn't leave. After I volunteered for just under a year, they decided to hire me as part-time staff. And that's how I got into animal rescue—through volunteering.

Volunteering is my way of giving back some of the unconditional love my dogs gave me growing up. A lot of us grow up with pets, and losing them is such a hard thing. It's not until after that chapter in our lives that we realize how much value our pets give us, how much joy and laughter. I volunteer to bring that joy to the world, one senior dog at a time, encouraging and reassuring them that they are safe, loved, and that there's warmth and goodness left in the world, just for them.

The reward of seeing the new dogs come in and quickly get adopted out—there's something about helping them through that process that keeps me going. And that's exactly it—it's a process. There's a cycle involved. A new animal comes in, and you have to assess them and give them certain types of care. At some point during that care, they are rehabilitated enough to adopt them out. In less than three years, I've seen close to one thousand dogs get adopted through Muttville. I think getting exposed to the field, the day-to-day operations of animal rescue, is what keeps me coming back.

Picasso Finds a Home

Like many scared or abused dogs, Picasso had a hard time in the shelter. His anxiety and fear continued even when he was removed from the shelter by the wonderful volunteers at Muttville Senior Dog Rescue, and that fear made such a loving dog seem like a lot to handle for a potential adopter. Thankfully, Picasso finally found safety and friendship when he was adopted by a longtime Muttville volunteer named Sara Stroud. Here is Sara's story:

I used to volunteer with Muttville. One weekend I took my boyfriend, Lloyd, to an open house so he could meet all the dogs. There was a gated area in front with a bunch of adoptable Muttville dogs. As soon as we walked up, Picasso greeted us and crawled into my lap. That was sort of it.

Now he lives a very dynamic existence between San Francisco and Berkeley. Picasso and I get up early in the morning and drive across the bridge to Lloyd's house. We all have coffee together at six thirty a.m. Then I go off to work, and Lloyd takes Picasso to his woodshop in Alameda, where he has lots of cozy little sleeping spots. In the evening we all reconvene in San Francisco. It's a pretty busy life.

He was actually considered one of their more challenging dogs. Right before we adopted him, Muttville's director, Sherri, asked us if we wanted an easier dog. I said no, we wanted the right dog. He can be a handful—he's dog

anything is possible

reactive and barks a lot—but we took him to special classes for that and now he's doing a lot better. It's still pretty hard when people come over, because it takes a while for Picasso to stop barking at them. It's doable, though. It just requires a little bit of patience. He's really grown by leaps and bounds, and that's very encouraging.

Both my parents died not long before I adopted Picasso. That's a lot for a small dog to take on. He's become an anchor for me and helped me create a new family. That's been a really huge part of healing my broken heart. He's like a bonding agent that has brought Lloyd and me even closer and turned us all into a family unit. The majority of the time, we're just laughing and talking about Picasso because he's such a delight to be around. I can't overstate how wonderful it's been to adopt him.

I would never consider getting a non-shelter dog. There's something really healing about being around the senior dogs in particular. Their calmness and demeanor allow for a slightly more relaxed lifestyle. Picasso likes to walk, but because he's older, he doesn't need to run miles and miles every day. That was really appealing, as was the prospect of saving a loving creature that might have otherwise been unwanted. Adopting Picasso is one of the best choices we ever made. I feel so lucky to get to be his friend and caretaker, and I am so thankful and appreciative to everyone at Muttville for rescuing him and loving him until we met him.

PAWSITIVE TAILS
CERTIFICATE OF TRAINING

Presented to

Pico

for successfully completing
Drama Queens & Divas
Dec 23, 2014

VOLUNTEERS Rachel Zink and Alisha Kavey

DOG Poppa

RESCUE GROUP Berkshire Humane Society (Pittsfield, Massachusetts)

Alisha: I started volunteering after I got injured and couldn't work anymore. I needed to help somebody. Then Rachel got interested in it, and we started coming together. Now we volunteer once a week, and we're also on call.

Rachel: I wanted to volunteer because I love dogs, and we can't have dogs in our apartment. I used to have a dog, but she ended up with my ex, which was really tough. I feel like I gave her up, like I abandoned her. There are so many dogs that need love at the shelter—I figured I might as well go help those dogs since I don't have a dog of my own anymore.

Alisha: We love working together—that's actually how we met, while on the same job. We just clicked really well. We figured if we could work together, we could certainly volunteer together.

Rachel: It's always fun to see the new dogs come in. They've all got different personalities, and they all look different, just like people. It feels good to help an organization that needs the help. It would clearly cost too much money to run this shelter without volunteers.

Alisha: I know that if we're doing something like helping with the laundry or taking the dogs for walks, it frees up the staff to actually do something that's useful, like work with a dog that's struggling or work with the public to help get the dogs out. If we can take some of that burden off of them—the little things, the things that we can do—then everybody is working together like a puzzle and we're all part of the team.

VOLUNTEER Sean Lanham

DOG Blondie

RESCUE GROUP El Paso Animal Services (El Paso, Texas)

I'm part of the Very Irresistible Pets program here. We take dogs that are social, healthy, and good with kids and give them extra attention and support so that they can get adopted. The goal is to find these animals homes, to keep them safe and taken care of in case their owners come back for them. When animals come in here, the object is not so much to get rid of them but to get them back out to their owners, to find them good homes, good people who want them. The VIP program is a big part of that.

I've been volunteering every Saturday for about four months now. I'm currently in a facility—a halfway house for probationees. I was given the opportunity to come out here and volunteer with the dogs. It's a community service program, but it's also therapeutic. I guess I've been doing well, because I get to keep coming back.

Next Saturday is going to be my last Saturday as a volunteer, because I'm getting released from my facility. But I'm going to apply to work out here, see if maybe I can be a kennel attendant, so that I can still be with the dogs.

Some mornings I wake up and just because of, you know, life at the moment—being away from home, being in an institution, being away from my family—I'm not always in the best of moods. Sometimes I'm just mad at the world. I can come out here and work around these dogs for five, ten minutes, and suddenly I'm in a good mood. My mind is just focused on working with them and getting them out. I feel like I'm saving a life, because I am. They put a smile on my face, kind of warm me up on the inside, and make me appreciative.

VOLUNTEER Ashley Niels

DOG Hilda

RESCUE GROUP Austin Animal Services (Austin, Texas)

I'm a huge rescue animal person. I'm always finding strays anyway and keeping them until I adopt them out. I started fostering animals here in 2011 when they moved into this new facility. They were doing renovations, and they wanted to get the animals out of the shelter and into foster homes to make the process less stressful for them. I signed up and was going to take home a small, healthy animal, but went home with a big kitty with kennel cough.

Now I volunteer here in addition to fostering. Volunteering can be hard, especially when your favorites go home—that's always bittersweet. But I love them. It's not even that I like them. I love them like my own. And I come back because I make a difference.

What I try to do is pick one or two animals during my shift and really work with them one-on-one. I especially like working with the shy ones. This can be a pretty overwhelming place, and even though the Austin Animal Center is awesome, it's still loud. I help bring the shy ones around, and I try to get them to trust other people. That can make the difference between them being adopted or not. If they're scared in their kennel, nobody can see them.

You can't be unhappy when you're here with them. These animals make me smile when I walk up to them as they wag their tails and show me they're happy to see me. It just fills me up with happiness. I want these animals to know what it's going to be like when they're in their forever home. I want them to know what love and hope are so they're prepared for it.

VOLUNTEER Janiya England

DOG Demetri

RESCUE GROUP Used Dogs Rescue (New Orleans, Louisiana)

I've been volunteering since I was four. I'm ten now. I volunteer because I really like dogs—they're just so adorable. I like to take care of them. It makes me feel like I'm a hero to the dogs because I'm helping them. I'm feeding them, and I'm giving them walks and water, and taking care of them so they can be healthy and they can get adopted.

I think I've learned that dogs can be different, like humans, and they can be alike, like humans. Some dogs don't like the heat, like people do, and some dogs like the heat. Or they might not like the cold, and some people don't like the cold. They practically eat the same food as we do, but theirs is not cooked, and it's ground up. Our food is just cooked and whole. They have to take almost the same kind of medicine as we do, because they can get colds, too. They can even get cancer, like humans do. I think I'll be working with dogs forever, just because I love them. They're just beautiful to me. Being with them is just a beautiful thing to me.

VOLUNTEER Emily Conn

DOG Sassy

RESCUE GROUP Used Dogs Rescue (New Orleans, Louisiana)

I've been volunteering about two years, since I was twelve. When I met Janiya, we became instant friends, of course, and now she's like a little sister to me. Then I met Madalin, and she asked if I wanted to start volunteering with the dogs. I said, "Yeah, I love dogs."

I didn't really know what to expect when I started. I'm happy for the dogs because their lives were really bad before they got rescued. I'm learning that volunteering is not all about yourself—it's about helping and giving and learning how to take care of these dogs that were in horrible positions before we got them. I actually really like working with dogs. I think I'll do it forever. I was thinking about being a veterinarian at one point, and if I don't go into a career with dogs, maybe I can just continue volunteering.

VOLUNTEERS Barbara McKinney, deAnne Guarino, Lucy Guarino, and Joe Guarino

DOGS Biscuit and Jo

RESCUE GROUP Montgomery Humane Society (Montgomery, Alabama)

Barbara: I think it's important that the kids understand how to give back, and that you always stand up for the little people.

Joe: It's character building. The dogs have been a part of our entire lives, so it's nice to come back and make their week a little better for what they've done for us.

Lucy: It's also nice to see a dog that's been here for a really long time find a home.

Joe: It's satisfying. You know that when you come down here and run around and let the dogs get some of that energy out, they'll act like normal dogs around people. That makes a difference in people's eyes. Dogs don't always act the way they normally would when they're in a cage. You have to free them a bit first before people can really see the dog.

Barbara: It helps them adjust to other dogs, as well.

Lucy: The shelter sends out a list of who gets adopted every week, and Grandma's not always on the Internet, so we'll call each other and say, "So-and-so got adopted!" We work really hard with those dogs to try and get them to understand that this is okay, this place is okay, we're okay, you're okay.

Barbara: And life will be better.

Lucy: Once those dogs get adjusted to shelter life, it gives them a chance to get adopted. And when that dog gets adopted, it's a big deal at our house. Across, you know . . .
Across three generations.

the dogs

Many dogs lose their way and come upon hard times for countless reasons. But the one thing that unites these abandoned animals is their unending ability to love. They wake up inside the shelter every morning ready to give and receive love, ready to forgive and move forward, ready for their second chance. It is the unstoppable positive energy of a shelter dog that makes them creatures like no other. Animal shelters may be full of sad stories, but behind each sad story is an incredible tale of survival and love.

DOG Gwen

VOLUNTEER Schyler Goodrich

RESCUE GROUP Berkshire Humane Society (Pittsfield, Massachusetts)

Gwen came up from the Atlanta Humane Society. Because she had a little bit of a cold, she was quarantined for a couple of weeks. Now she's healthy and is in the general population, so potential adopters can see her. She's interacting very well with other dogs, and she loves people. Nobody's shown any interest in adopting her yet. She looks a little older than she is, which I think dissuades people. She's only six, but she has that older gray look.

People are hesitant to adopt an older dog because they know that animal may be with them for only a short time. I think that's why the older dogs tend to stick around here a bit longer. It really depends on the dog, and the karma, and what somebody's looking for at that time. A lot of it is fate.

We had a dog that was here for a year and half, and she finally got adopted out. Now she's at a place with a lake and a dock, and her owner loves her. We knew she was an amazing dog, but she just needed to find the right home. It's special when we see those dogs go, because a shelter life is not a life. Oftentimes the adopters will send us photos of how the dogs are doing, so we can see that they're happy. It's just an awesome feeling.

DOG Maude

VOLUNTEER Amberly Crawford

RESCUE GROUP Montgomery Humane Society (Montgomery, Alabama)

Maude's been here for a little over a year now. Maybe almost two years. She was healthy and up for adoption, and then one day the volunteers were doing a photo shoot outside with her and she wouldn't get up. They took her to the doctor and found she had a heart murmur. She's on medicine now, and the doctor recently gave her a clean bill of health. They didn't hear or see the heart murmur.

The staff around here really loves the animals and wants to save all of them. They kept Maude in the office, away from the other dogs that were up for adoption, while she was going through treatment and trying to get better. The staff just let her stay. Everybody who comes into the office knows Maude, even the volunteers. "Oh, we gotta go see Maude," they say. "We talked to Maude today."

Maude loves treats, so she expects everybody to bring her a treat. You can tell. She's a product of a lot of treats.

DOG McCoy

VOLUNTEER Jenna Turk

RESCUE GROUP Big Fluffy Dog Rescue (Nashville, Tennessee)

McCoy came out of a very bad hoarding case here in Tennessee. There were many, many dogs on the property that were already dead by the time rescuers got there. He was horribly emaciated and in terrible shape. He weighed only fifty pounds at intake. This dog should weigh more than ninety pounds. Because he was in such terrible condition, they aged him at ten years old. I don't think there's any way that he's ten, because I see him play now. He's much younger than that, but his teeth are very bad from being malnourished. Before he was rescued, he was chewing on anything, trying to eat whatever he could find. My family's been fostering him a little over a month. We take him for weekly weight checks to see how much he's gaining, and we spoil him with special food. Basically, he gets anything he wants right now.

It will be a while before he makes the main adoption page and becomes available, because they're going to do some physical therapy for his backside. His hips are a little wonky, so they want to do water therapy for him. I just asked if I would still have him at Thanksgiving, and Jean (Big Fluffy Dog Rescue's director) said, "Probably." I asked that because my mom and stepdad are going to be in town, and I want them to meet him.

This dog has seen hell, and he's come out the other side. And I get to be a part of that recovery. When we started fostering him, he wouldn't come to us for attention. We had to go to him. Now he'll come up and nudge you. He wants that love, and he wants that attention. It just makes you feel good to see that.

McCoy Finds a Home

After starting his life as a victim of a hoarding situation, McCoy finally found comfort and safety within his foster home. He was so well taken care of and so deeply loved by his foster family that when the time came for McCoy to choose a proper forever home, it's no wonder he didn't have to look very far. Here's rescuer Jenna Turk's story:

McCoy is doing great, though, actually, we got a really bad diagnosis last Thursday after he had been limping for a while. The vet says it is osteosarcoma. He has a tumor in his right leg. The treatment is either amputation or chemotherapy. His back end simply isn't strong enough to support just three legs, and frankly, I don't want to put him through chemo. It's so hard on the dog. I went to another vet for a second opinion, and they told me that I'd have to put him to sleep right away. I said that there was no way that I could do that to my kids.

They just love him so much. So we decided that we'd put him on medication until we simply can't anymore.

Now I watch him like a hawk. When I see that he is not putting any weight on his foot at all, it's going to be time to say goodbye. Right now he's smiling and happy, and there is no pain in his eyes. The day will come, though, when we'll all need to say goodbye, because I can't bear to see him in any pain.

I usually foster puppies with Big Fluffy. McCoy was my first adult dog foster. When he came to us, he was so broken. I took my youngest son in the

car with me to pick him up—he was only three at the time—and he looked at him and said, "Momma, why is he so bumpy? And why are his eyes so sad?"

I told him, "Baby, those are his bones. He needs to eat a lot of good food, and we're gonna fix those bumps and we're gonna make his eyes happy." I don't really know the whole story of what McCoy has been through, but I do know that he was in a hoarding case. Two of the dogs he was with did not survive the first night after rescue. That's how far gone they were. So my family really got to take that journey with him, see him gain weight, see him get stronger, and see those lumps and bumps go away. They got to see that sadness in his eyes disappear.

He quickly realized that this was in a safe place and that people loved him. This is home for him. He gets away with things that the other dogs don't get away with because he's special. He's allowed to beg when we have dinner. Almost everybody gives him something off their plate. He's allowed to steal food and never gets in trouble. He's really just such a sweet dog, and it breaks my heart to think about what he went through. It breaks my heart knowing he has to go through this bone cancer now.

After I took him to the vet last week, we both got cheeseburgers on the way home. That's something I've always done with him from the very first car ride we ever took; we stopped and got cheeseburgers. Until the time comes, I'll cater to him and do whatever he needs me to do. We were really the only family he ever knew, so at least now he can be with us. I'm going to do everything I can to make sure he stays comfortable for as long as possible.

DOG Pollydoodle

VOLUNTEER Ron Dischert

RESCUE GROUP Austin Animal Services (Austin, Texas)

Pollydoodle's been in and out of here a few different times. I was involved with her original adoption, but that was a little bit iffy. It was to an older woman who loved Pollydoodle, but she just couldn't handle her on leash. Unfortunately, she had to return her to the shelter, but she'd come visit her on a regular basis. At first I thought she was trying to take her back. I don't think that would have been a good idea.

Other than that ten-day stint, Polly's been with us for two years. Since this past April she's been boarded off-site because she's so stressed here at the animal center. She only gets out of her crate to go potty four times a day. But we do have really good volunteers, who take her home and do overnights with her. I actually just picked her up today from another volunteer who had her for an overnight visit.

She hasn't really had any other potential adopters, so the director is going to do a push and help me get her adopted. She's doing surprisingly well, though. Better than we volunteers are doing, if that makes sense. We just really want to get her adopted and get her into a good home.

DOG Poppa

VOLUNTEERS Rachel Zink and Alisha Kavey

RESCUE GROUP Berkshire Humane Society (Pittsfield, Massachusetts)

Poppa's been here at least a month. Obviously, I think he'd be doing better if he were in a home, but as far as the shelter goes, he's doing pretty well. Some of the dogs come in and they just can't handle it, but Poppa's strong.

Our area's really good for pit bulls because people have a lot of land and aren't so prejudiced against them. People here just don't seem to be fazed by pit bulls. It seems like in the cities, nobody wants to have a pit bull around because of the stereotypes. I think it's all about how they're raised—and that goes for any kind of dog.

When Poppa first came in, he was very scared of men. Although we don't know what that's from, exactly, we think he might have been abused in the past. Now he's doing a lot better with everybody. He listens pretty well and he's super lovable.

DOG Svetta

VOLUNTEER Lennie Hammit

RESCUE GROUP McKinley County Humane Society (Gallup, New Mexico)

Svetta came in with six other puppies—five girls and two boys. Finn and Jake are the two boys. There's Svetta, Peewee, Sweetness, Fiona, Sienna, Jake, and Finn. We named them all. Mama's name was already Sandy. We let her keep her name. You know what? If I went into the dog pound, I would want to keep my identity, too. She's really sweet.

I think maybe the grandkids bred her, and then it just got to be too much and they couldn't take care of her. So then they dumped her and the litter of puppies off at the grandparents' house. Then the grandpa came to the shelter. He had a nice-looking truck, shiny and brand-new with black side rails. He said, "I have these puppies, and I need to bring them in."

Usually we ask a donation of fifteen dollars when somebody surrenders an animal, just to give them their first vaccination. He donated ninety dollars. When he went outside to bring the puppies in, he asked me if they were going to be okay. I told him, "Sure, we'll take care of them. They're gonna find a home, you know." I told him that if we adopt them out, they'll get spayed and neutered before they leave. No one's allowed to adopt a dog from our shelter without getting them fixed first. It's really nice to see that a lot of people care and want to make sure these animals get into a good home, even if they can't keep them.

Grandpa was happy when he heard that. Everybody was happy. We had pretty little puppies to take care of, and they're so cute. I always pick a favorite one out of the bunch, and this one's my favorite. That puppy breath, though.

DOG George

VOLUNTEER Katie Hemphill

RESCUE GROUP Used Dogs Rescue (New Orleans, Louisiana)

About three years ago we were adopting out a dog when we noticed a dog next door. He was all worn down, tied outside to a very short chain, and stepping in his own poop. We gently asked the owner about the situation and offered to take George off his hands. However, the owner refused to surrender him. Apparently, George's owner would peer over his fence every day and watch the adopted dog happily coming out of its shell, living a good life and running free. Finally, after five months, George's owner called us up and said he couldn't keep his dog chained up anymore, so we picked George up. We have had him ever since.

He used to be scared of everything, but he's gotten so much better. He's the epitome of a dog that's been freed. When he's in the yard, he's like a bunny, bouncing and rolling and joyful. It's amazing to watch. He's pretty dog aggressive, though, which has made it hard to find him a forever home.

George Finds a Home

Like many pit bull–type dogs, George was mislabeled "dog aggressive," which made it hard for him to find a forever home. Even though everyone was root-

ing for him, he struggled with fear issues that came from his earlier neglect, and some people thought he might never be able to live as a family dog. But sometimes all it takes is that one perfect person to cross a dog's path and change his life forever. Thankfully, that happened to George when he came to live with Tammy Pimley. Here's Tammy's story:

A friend of mine had been fostering George for a while around Christmas, and I saw her post a picture of him on her Facebook page. I thought he looked adorable, but I needed to know if he was good with kids. Someone from Used Dogs got in touch with me and said that he was actually amazing with kids, so we set up a time to go visit him. He *was* amazing. We were ready to take him home right then, but the volunteers wanted to visit our home first to make sure it was a safe space for George.

At the time, we only had a four-foot fence around our yard, and Used Dogs thought that George would be able to jump right over it and escape. We really wanted to adopt him, but I just couldn't afford a new fence. The kids were heartbroken, as I was. Then one of the volunteers said she knew some people who might be willing to fix my fence. The next week three guys showed up and

built me a new fence so George could have a nice, secure place to live. Used Dogs paid for the whole thing. I wouldn't have been able to do that on my own. It was such a blessing.

I knew that George came from a really bad environment. Before getting rescued, he had lived for years on a chain without room to even walk around. Now he's loving and affectionate, especially with the kids. He's come so far.

I think my kids have learned a lot from him about resilience and about not letting circumstances define you. He's such a happy and joyful dog, and he's willing to give people a second chance. Even in my own relationships, I know that once you get hurt, you don't know if you'll ever be able to trust again. But it seems like dogs don't have that same hesitation; they're just eager to love and be loved.

George nudges my baby every morning to wake her up, and she wraps her arms around him and loves him. I think it helps my son to have another man in the house, because he's the only boy. George is his buddy now. They hang out and go on walks. It's kind of guy time, I guess. He's an incredible addition to our family. I don't think that any other dog would have been as perfect.

Every day I'm amazed by him. After being chained up for so many years, he loves being in the backyard. Sometimes he'll stay out there all night, running around and having the most fun of his entire life. We're all just so glad we found him.

DOG Name Unknown

VOLUNTEER Juan Mora

RESCUE GROUP El Paso Animal Services (El Paso, Texas)

I hardly ever read their kennel cards. I don't want to fall in love with them, just in case they get put down. You know, it hurts me. I know that this dog came in as a stray two days ago, and I'm going to try my best to find him a home. Some dogs come in already microchipped, so you assume that their owners are going to come for them. I've heard too many stories about people just leaving their dogs tied up against a fence. People will pick them up and bring them here. I tell the people who come in, "You know, this is a major responsibility. You might as well think it over before you adopt them." Being honest with a person means that I can make them feel more at ease about adopting a dog.

I've helped twenty-four dogs get adopted over the past two months. I tell my daughter, "Baby, you know how many dogs have a new home?" She says, "How many, Daddy?" I tell her, and she's like, "Yay, I'm proud of you, Daddy!" I brought her over here, and she asked me, "Are they gonna wake up again?" I said, "No." She understands that they're going to put them to sleep. Sometimes you see a little tear, but she gets so happy when I tell her, "You know what, I got five of them out today."

DOG Miller

VOLUNTEER Cindy Ross

RESCUE GROUP The Little Guild of Saint Francis
(West Cornwall, Connecticut)

I think Miller's popular because he's a very likable dog. I see him as the kind of dog that would love to ride around with a guy in a pickup truck, stroll around in the woods and get all dirty and gross, and then hang out in a lodge somewhere by the fire. My daughter was thinking about adopting him, but that didn't end up working out even though she liked him a lot. Miller was actually the first dog that I ever walked. He was very easy, and that's what made me keep coming back. These dogs are happy here; this is their home, and I think that speaks volumes about how adaptable and loving they are. They are just so willing to respond to love.

DOG Robbie

VOLUNTEER Cheyenne Yazzie

RESCUE GROUP McKinley County Humane Society (Gallup, New Mexico)

I was going home one day when I saw someone in a black truck throw this puppy out of the window. I thought the dog was dead. I pulled over. He was lying on his side, completely traumatized. When I went over there, he freaked out on me. Luckily, I had dog food in my car. When he saw that, he just ran up and ate the dog food like it was nothing. I took him home, and all he did for days was sleep on my lap. I'm fostering him right now, and I plan on putting him on transport soon. I know it will be hard to say goodbye to him. I feel like I bonded more with him because I was the one who rescued him. He could have died right there. Someone could have run him over, or he could have easily starved to death. But I stopped because I thought maybe he could still be alive, maybe he needed help and I could give him that help, and maybe he could have a loving home and I could provide that for him.

DOG Bear

VOLUNTEER Michelle Pekrol

RESCUE GROUP Berkshire Humane Society (Pittsfield, Massachusetts)

Bear's a great dog—an Australian shepherd mix, which means he has herding tendencies. He's going to need a home with some space and an active lifestyle. He's not going to be a dog that can sit on the couch all day. He's really soft, and he's very sweet. I think he'll do okay here at the shelter because the volunteers go in and spend time with each dog and make sure they're all doing okay.

We had a dog named Kingsley that was here for a year and a half. He was in a kennel in the back of the shelter, and I spent a lot of time with him. I started this project called "The Kingsley Chronicles" where we took him around town, trying to get him adopted at various events. I told our kennel staff that I thought Kingsley was actually depressed being in a kennel in the back. I suggested that maybe we could move him up to one of the suites in the front where he could have some natural light and more exposure. So they did, and his attitude changed completely. He finally got adopted out to the right home. Because the volunteers and staff spend so much time with these animals, they react right away if they see something wrong.

DOG Oreo

VOLUNTEER Kristin Morris

RESCUE GROUP Austin Animal Services (Austin, Texas)

Oreo is awfully cute and very calm. He's seven now, and came to the shelter as an owner surrender. He seems like a dog that would fit in very well with a family. It's kind of hard to see—he'd been with somebody probably his entire life, and then they just weren't able to keep him anymore. But I think he'll do well here. He does have seizures, but he doesn't seem to have any other health problems. If we could just find somebody who would be willing to give him medication, he'd be all set. He walks very nicely, and he seems like he'd be a pretty easy dog to train.

DOGS Maggie and her puppies Rolo and Whopper

VOLUNTEER Heather Dineen

RESCUE GROUP The Little Guild of Saint Francis
(West Cornwall, Connecticut)

Maggie came up from our partner shelter in Tennessee, and she was very pregnant. We tried to get someone to foster her before she had her puppies, but no one came forward.

On Mother's Day she gave birth to five little babies here in the shelter, all named after different types of candy. They are so cute. She is such a sweet dog. She is an amazing mom and deserves the best home. Once her babies are weaned and she goes through heartworm treatment, Maggie will be up for adoption, as well. We all hope she finds a great home because she is so sweet, but pit bulls sit at the shelter longer, unfortunately. She's obviously been through a lot and had many, many litters of puppies. It will be good for her to finally be done with that. Before she leaves the shelter, she'll be spayed. This is the last litter she'll have to care for, thankfully.

DOG Joey

VOLUNTEER Paige Gruda

RESCUE GROUP McKinley County Humane Society (Gallup, New Mexico)

This puppy was found in a box on Interstate 40, on the side of the road. He was the only one, as far as we know. There could've been more, but the birds could've gotten them. When people finally pulled over and grabbed the box, there were birds circling. So maybe he had been thrown out with a few other puppies, but he was the only one that survived. Some Good Samaritans saved him and brought the box into the shelter, and he'll be getting transported to a rescue group soon.

There are just so many dogs here in Gallup and on the reservation. I think he will have a much better chance at getting a home through a rescue out of state. He's a good puppy. He's a sweetheart. He loves being with people, and he loves being held. I think he's probably part Chihuahua and part blue heeler.

DOG Greta

VOLUNTEER Ellen Kallman

RESCUE GROUP Austin Animal Services (Austin, Texas)

Greta's been here for a couple weeks, which for her size is kind of a long time. I think that it's probably because she's over ten years old and she's visually impaired. She does have some sight, but you need to be cautious with her because she will walk into things. This center waives the adoption fee for dogs over seven years old. And she comes with a free, brand-new bed! So there are some things we do to encourage adopters, but really, we just hope that people will adopt our animals because it feels good, not just because it's free.

We've got a lot of puppies right now in the shelter. People see Greta and say, "Oh, how cute," and then right next to her is this darling little puppy. It's hard. And yes, a lot of people want puppies. So she needs to find the right home, and that makes her adoption a little more difficult than an adoption for a puppy or a one- or two-year-old dog. She is spayed, though. A lot of people don't realize that is a plus, because you can take her right away. But I'm not going to lie. The age goes against them. It just does, even though it really shouldn't. They can be wonderful pets when they're this old and trained.

DOG Henry

VOLUNTEER Katie Hemphill

RESCUE GROUP Used Dogs Rescue (New Orleans, Louisiana)

Henry is about six years old. Unfortunately, he's been with us a while because of his issue with water. When he hears a hose or running water, he gets really upset, which makes him harder to adopt out. It is actually pretty common. People down here will punish their dogs by spraying them with a hose when they're barking or doing something "bad," or their kids will grab a hose and torture the dog. Clearly, something happened, but that's really the only challenge he has. If there was somebody that was willing to work on that with him, it would be a great fit.

DOG Curry

VOLUNTEER Rachel Price

RESCUE GROUP Animal Care and Control Team Philly
(Philadelphia, Pennsylvania)

Curry came in about three weeks ago. He's about eight to ten years old. He came in as a stray, which is interesting. Normally, older, breed-specific dogs like him are not your typical stray dogs. He's clearly well fed, and he was probably somebody's pet.

People sometimes just let their dog go, or if the dogs get out, they just think, oh well. Sometimes dogs are found as strays, and people tell us, "Oh, I didn't want him anyway." We get the saddest surrender reasons.

Curry's really sweet. He just wants to sit on your lap and eat snacks. He'd be good for an older person. I've been his advocate. I've sent him to a few rescues and put him online. I love how many rescues we work with here. It really feels like you're actually doing something to move a dog through the system. He's an easy dog, and he's great with other dogs.

Curry Finds a Home

Curry was a staff favorite at the shelter, which meant he had a lot of volunteers shining a spotlight on him. At a busy, city-run shelter, this makes an incredible difference. Because of his wonderful demeanor and the support of his favorite volunteers, Curry quickly found his way into the arms of Kali Taylor and her partner. This is Kali's story:

My partner and I adopted Curry on October 4, 2015. It was his fifth birthday, according to shelter records. He fits right into our family because we're all a bit older, so we have our good days and then we have our days when we just need to be couch potatoes. There are a lot of animals that don't have homes in Philly, especially older animals, and my heart goes out to them because the younger ones always get adopted first. Curry's age was an important reason why I wanted to get to know him, because some of those older dogs never get a chance to leave the shelter at all.

He had kennel cough when we adopted him, so my partner and I nursed him back to health. I think he real-

ized this was his forever home two or three months after being adopted. Now he's just so comfortable. We spoil him. He loves his rubs and his food and his walks, and when we can, we'll rent a car and take him on the road and let him stretch out and run somewhere outside the city. The shelter said that they found Curry roaming the streets before they picked him up, so we know that he has some anxiety about living in a loud city. We're working on that with him. He's inspired us to petition the city to create a new dog park in our neighborhood, because we don't have a lot of resources in Southwest Philly for our pets. We want Curry and his friends to have a safe, clean place to play in.

Having an animal will teach you some things. I've learned to relax my OCD, and I've watched my partner form her own special bond with Curry, which has been so beautiful. We both feel very fortunate that he's in our lives. The shelter was having an adoption special the day we met him, which meant all adoption fees had been lowered. It turned out that the staff and volunteers loved Curry so much and wanted him to find a home so badly that they ended up waiving the entire adoption fee for us. The volunteers said that they had a really good feeling about my partner and me, so maybe we didn't find Curry that day. Maybe he found us.

DOG Brianna

VOLUNTEER Lisa Hart

RESCUE GROUP Big Fluffy Dog Rescue (Nashville, Tennessee)

Brianna was a stray that Big Fluffy pulled from a very underfunded shelter in Georgia. She had a mammary tumor. It appears that she probably had been overbred by a backyard breeder. At eighteen months old she's easily had more than one litter of puppies. I don't know if she was sick when I started fostering her, but her coat was in terrible condition. It was sparse and wiry, and you could see right through to her skin. Every bone showed. She was just a throwaway dog. She would have been killed at the other shelter if we hadn't rescued her.

It took me probably five weeks to get her to take a treat from my hand. Understandably, she didn't trust people. It didn't matter how good the treat was. She wasn't going to take the chance that I would hurt her. That just broke our hearts, watching her like that. But now, she takes a treat. She's learned that people are good and not to be afraid, that people offer good things like pats, reliable food and water, and fun, too. She's not a big player, but she has fun running out in the yard, chasing things, and barking at birds. She's just enjoying life, basically.

DOG Turbo

VOLUNTEER Traci Herndon

RESCUE GROUP Montgomery Humane Society (Montgomery, Alabama)

Turbo's been here less than a year. He's three years old, and he came in as a stray. We don't know anything about him, except that he arrived with the number four drawn on both sides of his back and legs with a super-durable permanent marker. It's just recently faded. I don't know if the shelter employees have been washing him every week or not, but it was on there for a long, long time. I felt like it was a huge deterrent to potential adopters. Nobody wanted a dog with a four on him, you know? We think that maybe he was a fighting dog or a racing dog, and that he broke loose and ran away. Maybe they just dumped him. Maybe he lost or didn't do right. He's a little skittish. I would imagine it's from his background.

He's a great walker, with a good gait. I usually walk two dogs at a time because there are so many that need to go out. I walk about thirty dogs in three hours. I can walk him with any other dog. He never bothers the other dog, never yips at them, never does anything.

Turbo hasn't had any potential adopters, though. Ms. Chapman, our volunteer coordinator, sends out a newsletter every Tuesday letting us all know who helped which dog, what's going on, and who got adopted. The volunteers often text each other to say, "Turbo got a visit today!" But there's never been news of an adoption—hopefully soon, though. He's just a great dog.

DOG Abbott

VOLUNTEER Katy Sharp

RESCUE GROUP Big Fluffy Dog Rescue (Nashville, Tennessee)

Abbott came from Sylacauga, which is an extremely poverty-stricken town in southern Alabama. All the industrial companies moved out several years ago, and people just abandoned their homes, not to mention their unspayed and unneutered pets. Dogs run rampant there. It's like the Chernobyl of unspayed animals.

The ladies who asked Big Fluffy to get involved and help the Sylacauga dogs had actually taken pictures of them a week before we got there. They told us, "They're really scared. We hope you can catch all these dogs while you're here. They look ill." Thankfully, we were able to, and it's been awesome. Abbott is recovering well, and he's one of my favorites.

DOG Baby Blue

VOLUNTEER Cheryl McClure

RESCUE GROUP McKinley County Humane Society (Gallup, New Mexico)

I was at Red Rock State Park, which is just east of McKinley. We were tailgating, and this little stray puppy was just kind of hanging out with us. I spoke with one of the campers who had been there for several days. He said that he'd been feeding and watering the dog but that the dog didn't belong to him. I said, "You know, I volunteer with the shelter, and I could take him in." That's how I ended up with him.

I brought him into the shelter and got him all his shots. We called him Baby Blue right away, because he's a puppy and he has incredibly beautiful blue eyes.

When we saw him, it was evident from the hair around his neck that he had been wearing a collar. I have a feeling somebody just took the collar off and dropped him off in the park. When I got him home, I think I might've figured out what the problem was. He would jump on you, and in his excitement he would pee. I have a feeling that some family knew how wonderful he was, but they weren't able to put up with the behavior. Since that time he's really calmed down, and I've only had him for a week.

This dog's sort of stolen my heart. Right away he was just very personable, and I hate to say this, but . . . he's pretty. I've fostered some mangy animals, as well, and I've loved them and cared for them just as much, but this one does have my heart. It's going to be hard to see him move on. But I know he's going to land well. So while it's hard, it's just what we do. We take them for a while, make sure they're healthy, and then move them on.

DOG Lucky

VOLUNTEER Pauline Clark

RESCUE GROUP Berkshire Humane Society (Pittsfield, Massachusetts)

Lucky definitely did not have a healthy past. She has touch sensitivities and is very submissive. She's also sensitive to sound and motion and will lie as flat as a pancake on the ground when she's scared, which is very sad. If you raise your hand to put something up on the wall, she panics and runs away, and she's always anxious on walks. She loves people, though, and the volunteers are helping her build confidence by socializing with her and teaching her to trust humans again.

I've never seen a dog leave here that hasn't been better than when it came in, especially those that are in really bad shape. The animals are just transformed. They leave the shelter 20 or 30 percent better because of the training and care and love that people give them here.

DOG Fletcher

VOLUNTEERS Vern and Jean Simpson

RESCUE GROUP Big Fluffy Dog Rescue (Nashville, Tennessee)

Jean: We knew Fletcher was heartworm positive when we started fostering him at the end of April.

Vern: But we didn't know what his history was.

Jean: He'd been coughing the whole time we had him. It never ceased. Our local vet did a lung X-ray and said, "I think the dog has blasto. I've never treated one. They've always had to be put down because the treatment can be at least ten thousand dollars." So I said, "We'll take him back to Big Fluffy." We were just thinking, "What are we gonna do? We can't take him away from our grandchildren."

Vern: Hunting dogs especially will snoop around in wet swampy areas. That's where blasto lives. Blasto can lay dormant for months before it becomes active. Most dogs don't survive.

Jean: When we called Big Fluffy, Jean Harrison, the president, said to me, "Can you afford to take care of this dog?" I said, "Before this we could, but this is just too expensive." So she told me to sign him back over to Big Fluffy and they'd take care of him. Fletcher spent about five intense months at the vet hospital, all covered by Big Fluffy. He lost . . . what?

Vern: About fifteen pounds.

Jean: He was really, really sick. In December he finally got a clean bill of health. About three months ago, though, he started panting really heavily. He now has heart disease and high blood pressure, but, you know, we got him. We know we're making a big difference for him. And he's happy.

Vern: We adopted him.

Jean: We did.

DOG Chicken Little

VOLUNTEER Vanessa Fernandez

RESCUE GROUP Animal Rescue League of Boston (Boston, Massachusetts)

Chicken Little was found abandoned in the BJ's Wholesale parking lot in Dedham. We were unable to retrieve any footage of who abandoned her or find out why she ended up there. Because of the marks on her nose, we suspect her muzzle was taped or something was put on her to prevent her from barking that left terrible scars.

She was just health-cleared by our vet today and will go up for adoption on Thursday, which is phenomenal. She's been in the shelter for about three weeks because she was in such poor medical condition when she arrived. She rehabilitated much faster than we thought she would, so she's going to go straight up to our adoption area. It's a sad story turned amazing.

DOG Marbles

VOLUNTEER Sherry Stephens

RESCUE GROUP Austin Animal Services (Austin, Texas)

Marbles is three years old, and he's been here about twelve days now. He came in as a stray. He's very well adjusted, and he never cries in his cage. When I go into the kennel area to take a dog out and I try to decide which one, it's just torture. Should I take this dog because it's being really nice and quiet, or should I take this dog because it's screaming to get out? Should I reward the well-behaved dog, or should I take the one that seems needier? It's so tough. And then there are those dogs who won't even let you into their kennel because they're so scared.

Marbles is a perfect dog, though his look is . . . interesting. When I have to photograph a dog for their kennel card or their online profile, I think, "Oh no. What should I do? Should I try to not show the crooked teeth, or not show the creepy-looking eye?" But a lot of people love an underbite, and a lot of people want a dog with a different look. Some people are just very nurturing. They want a three-legged dog, or a dog who's blind, or a dog who's very old. There seems to be a dog for everybody, you know?

DOG Jacie

VOLUNTEER Lara Kelly

RESCUE GROUP Animal Care and Control Team Philly
(Philadelphia, Pennsylvania)

Jacie was a stray. She came in on July 5, a very popular time for strays to come to the shelter. For some reason she kind of flew under the radar for a while. There were a bunch of people who really liked her, but for whatever reason she wasn't catching the eye of adopters or rescues. And then she was wrongly labeled "not good with other dogs."

I took her on as our Pen Pal. The Pen Pal program was started at our shelter to help dogs that were struggling behaviorally. Dogs are teamed up with one or two volunteers who commit to getting them out multiple times a week. Normally, our dogs never really get walked. There are so many animals and just not enough volunteers to do it. The Pen Pal volunteers work on the dogs' training, take them off-site to events, and help promote them. We take them hiking, socialize them, and basically prepare them as much as possible to be adopted. We all want these dogs to succeed.

As our Pen Pal, Jacie has proven to be fabulous. Her fur is gorgeous. It's really soft. She knows "Sit," and she walks like a dream. You could walk her with your pinky. She's a big dog, and some people come in here looking for that. She's probably three to five years old.

Jacie is my seventy-sixth Pen Pal. All my Pen Pal dogs have been adopted, minus three or four that were pulled into a rescue group. I'd say the program really works.

DOG Butters

VOLUNTEER Edward Kenniston

RESCUE GROUP The Little Guild of Saint Francis
(West Cornwall, Connecticut)

Butters has been here since he was two months old, so he's grown up in our shelter. It's surprising that he's been here so long. Maybe it's because he is a pit bull. His legs are a little deformed, but I think it makes him cuter. He loves everyone. He loves kids; he loves other dogs; he loves everything. He's our go-to event dog. Butters knows "Sit" and "Down." He's a really fast learner and very smart. A lot of people have been interested in him, but when they meet him, for some reason, they don't end up adopting him. I have no idea why, because he is such a good dog.

DOG Sammy

VOLUNTEER Brett Dalzell

RESCUE GROUP Berkshire Humane Society (Pittsfield, Massachusetts)

Sammy is a sweet four-month-old puppy who came from Atlanta, Georgia, via our partnership with the Atlanta Humane Society. Because he was shipped up to us, not a lot is known about his background. He's just a really well-rounded dog. Right after he arrived, he was adopted by a great woman, but Sammy was returned almost two days later because her situation didn't allow him to stay. She was just heartbroken.

One of our staff members took notice of Sammy and really fell for him. Now he's doing great as her forever dog. He came in with a sibling puppy who also got adopted quite quickly. The puppies tend to go pretty fast. I feel for the senior dogs who stay a while. I think people are hesitant to adopt older dogs because they've already gone through the heartbreak of seeing a dog pass on and assume they're setting themselves up for heartbreak again by adopting a dog with only a few years left. I tend to find the seniors quite endearing. A lot of times they're already trained, and they're at that age where they just want to relax. For people like me who don't need to get out and jog every day, a senior dog is kind of ideal. Seven years old for any dog is considered "senior," but most small breeds potentially have another ten years of life left. It's the word "senior" that seems to scare people.

the shelters

I encourage you to get involved with any of the groups featured in this book, either by becoming a volunteer, donating, or adopting. You can find them here:

Animal Care and Control Team Philly (Philadelphia, Pennsylvania)
www.acctphilly.org

Animal Rescue League of Boston (Boston, Massachusetts)
www.arlboston.org

Austin Animal Services (Austin, Texas)
www.austinanimalcenter.org

BADRAP (Oakland, California)
www.badrap.org

Berkshire Humane Society (Pittsfield, Massachusetts)
www.berkshirehumane.org

Big Fluffy Dog Rescue (Nashville, Tennessee)
www.bigfluffydogs.com

Downey Animal Care Center (Los Angeles, California)
http://animalcare.lacounty.gov/wps/portal/acc

El Paso Animal Services (El Paso, Texas)
www.elpasotexas.gov/animal-services

Golden Retriever Club of Greater Los Angeles Rescue (Los Angeles, California)
www.grcglarescue.org

The Little Guild of Saint Francis (West Cornwall, Connecticut)
www.littleguild.org

McKinley County Humane Society (Gallup, New Mexico)
www.facebook.com/GallupShelter

Montgomery Humane Society (Montgomery Alabama)
www.montgomeryhumane.com

Muttville Senior Dog Rescue (San Francisco, California)
www.muttville.org

Used Dogs Rescue (New Orleans, Louisiana)
www.facebook.com/Useddogsnola

Wags and Walks Rescue (Los Angeles, California)
www.wagsandwalks.org

AMANDA BRAUNING

about the author

Jesse Freidin is one of America's leading fine art dog photographers, with work in more than one hundred private collections throughout the United States. His award-winning portraiture has been exhibited in galleries across the country, telling a contemporary story of companionship and love that truly honors the role dogs play in our modern lives.

He is the creator of three viral dog photography series: The Doggie Gaga Project (2010), When Dogs Heal (2015), and Finding Shelter (2016). His work has been featured in *Vogue, Cosmopolitan, The Huffington Post, Garden & Gun* magazine, *Four & Sons* magazine, and many more. He lives with his favorite dog, Pancake, a ten-year-old Boston terrier.

Jesse works with private dog photography clients nationwide. Learn more about his studio and commission process online: www.jessefreidin.com.

Or follow along:

Facebook: www.facebook.com/jessefreidinphoto
Instagram: @jessefreidin
Twitter: @jessefreidin